MW01614666

Tomorrow's Children:

Meeting the needs of multiracial and multiethnic children at home, in early childhood programs, and at school.

Francis Wardle, Ph. D.

Forward by Edith King, Professor of Educational
Sociology and Crosscultural Studies, University of Denver

Center for the Study of Biracial Children
2300 S. Krameria St.,
Denver, Colorado. 80222

Published by the Center for the Study of Biracial Children
2300 S. Krameria St., Denver, Colorado. 80222

© **Center for the Study of Biracial Children, 1999**

Printed by Citizen Printing, Fort Collins, Colorado
Supervisor, Robin Minot

Photographs, including the cover: Francis Wardle, Ph. D.
Book Design: Francis Wardle, Ph. D.

The purpose of the Center for the Study of Biracial Children:

To develop written materials that portray interracial and interethnic families and their children positively;

To develop visual materials that introduce mixed-race children and their families into mainstream American reality;

To educate schools, child care programs and professionals working with interracial and interethnic children and their families;

To provide accurate information about this population to the news media, policymakers and researchers;

To advocate for the rights of mixed-race families and their children, including the right to an accurate category on forms;

To provide consultation on biracial and biethnic identity development;

To provide advice to professionals conducting research on this population.

ISBN Catalog Number: 0-9669094-1-0

Printed in the United States of America

Contents

Day care and school
Working with the school and child care
Programs for high risk children
Travel
Working with professionals
Support all forms of diversity
Conclusion

Conclusion

Acknowledgments

This book is the product of my family's growth and evolution. Maia, Eirlys, Kealan and RaEsa, can all be seen within these pages - their spirit, uniqueness, gifts, and development towards full adulthood. Family life involves dynamics, discussion, negotiating and collective spirit: traditions, rituals, struggles and triumphs. Within the family racial labels, socially imposed limitations, and externally imposed expectations are meaningless. A secure, healthy, dynamic family allows all of us to challenge society's narrow-mindedness, prejudice, and need to limit and control others.

The contemporary interracial movement is made up of many such families and individuals, who have used their belief in the rightness of their cause to create support groups, internet sites, newsletters and conferences. I can't name them all, but they include Elizabeth and Ron Radcliffe, the late Sandy Campbell, the Dardens, Yvette and Daniel Hollis, Nancy Brown, Ramona Douglass, Maria Root, the Reverend Hartley, Marta Cruz-Janzen, Charles Byrd, and my dear friend Dr. Edith King.

But the overriding spirit behind this book is Ruth Benjamin-Wardle - my wife of over 20 years, whose security in her individual worth transcends all of society's small-minded constraints.

The title of this book, *Tomorrow's Children,* was first used as the heading for a series of columns I wrote for the interracial publication, *New People,* published by Dan and Yvette Hollis. I appreciate their permission for me to use it for the title of my book. Ross, my computer guru, Kealan, my second computer guru (I need two) and Jim Kelly, who helped finance this project.

Forward
Edith W. King

In this important contribution to the understanding of biracial and multiethnic identity, Dr. Francis Wardle, one of the foremost authorities on these issues, offers new insights and knowledge for parents, educators, and social work professionals. His impressive range of expertise and the lived experiences of two decades with his own biracial family provide the sources for his special knowledge. He infuses this ground breaking book with information and advice critical for parents, for educators, for all those in the helping professions entering the multicultural world of the 21st century. From years of teaching and administering in schools, consulting for family social work and mental health organizations, and personal experience with his own children, Francis Wardle believes that the attitudes the family holds toward an interracial/interethnic identity effect all members of the group, as well as the broader society. He asserts that all our children need competent parenting, skillful teaching, and full health services. However, in the support of interethnic children and families these endeavors are all the more essential for developing healthy individuals.

Francis Wardle clearly states that the purpose of this book is to help parents and teachers develop security, comfort and acceptance in rearing biracial and biethnic children. He urges parents to challenge those who believe the children must reject their European heritage. He recommends they insist multicultural education include and support a full biracial and multiethnic identity for individuals. Dr. Wardle's book has been written specifically to provide information and advice to interracial and interethnic parents and those parents who have adopted biracial children. This readership includes single parent families, blended families, foster parents, as well as teachers and other professionals working with these families. He believes that to succeed in postmodern society everyone must learn to function effectively within the dominant culture. But this does not mean that biethnic and biracial individuals have to reject a component of their heritage or believe that they are somehow inferior or need to hide some part of their lineage.

From his extensive work Wardle has observed how some interracial families have a tendency to react to neighborhood and community rejection by retreating into a small circle of close friends and family members, stay home most of the time or only socialize with other interracial and supportive friends. He cogently cautions against such behavior, urging these parents to reach out to the neighborhood and local community, advocating for their children and forcefully protesting injustices against interracial and interethnic people. In the initial section of the book readers will find valuable advice well organized and clearly presented in charts that summarize many issues that confront biological and adopted biracial and biethnic children and their family members.

Later in the volume Francis Wardle advises teachers to be particularly sensitive to biracial and biethnic children's needs. He suggests that teachers be persistent in demanding that early child-hood programs and schools, publishes of book and curriculum materials, and the wider media meet the needs of biracial children, multiethnic families, as well as the traditional minority families. As an educator he counsels that teachers should insist there are sessions in workshops and conferences on multicultural education and diversity that also address the unique needs of interracial families and biracial and biethnic children.

Historically in this country, myths and persuasive attitudes promulgated the idea that mixed-race people were destined to be failures in life, living on the edge of poverty, or turning to crime as a result of their mixed race heritage. In *Tomorrow's Children* Francis Wardle not only dispels these false images, he assures us, as husband and father of an interracial family, and as regarded educator, a biracial/interethnic existence is wholesome, natural, and unquestionably a widespread phenomena in America and throughout the world today.   Edith W. King, 1998

Introduction

When Ruth (my wife) was in the hospital with our first child, Maia, I picked out a birth announcement card at a local store. "I think you have the wrong cards," the lady at the counter proclaimed.

"Why .... what's wrong with them?" I responded in a confused voice.

"The baby on the card is brown," she said.

I glanced back at the card, and quickly responded, "Yes, I know," and then finished paying for them.

The birth of Maia was a struggle for both of us. She was our first child - so the whole childbirth experience was new and frightening. My Triumph sports car was in the shop, so we relied on Ruth's beat-up light blue VW Bug. It was the rainy season in Kansas City - heavy rains every day, with swollen rivers and the threat of flooding. The doctors at the hospital seemed almost hostile. And when they finally said Ruth would have to have a "C" section, one of the doctors had the gall to comment, "When you came in, I figured it would be a 'C' section!"

I'm sure they never believed we were married. They never did get Maia's name on her crib correct - eventually writing Benjamin (Ruth's last name) - obviously believing I was only an "interested observer." Ruth's mother and other relatives provided needed support, especially since my parents, living in an isolated religious community, were not able to be there.

Before the birth of our first child we argued a great deal about how to raise children. Our hottest debates were around behaviorism. Ruth's academic training stressed behavior techniques; mine was built around free schools, student choice, and developmental psychology. At the time of Maia's birth Ruth was finishing her master's degree in Special Education - a discipline that stresses behavioral techniques. I was teaching at an alternative free school.

But - with all our discussions about raising children - we never argued about how to raise biracial children. We assumed there is no difference between raising White, Black and biracial children. Maybe we assumed this because all of our academic classes never addressed the issue. Maybe we were naive. Maybe, at that time (late 1970s) the thinking still was that all children, regardless of culture, race and ethnicity, have the same needs, and therefore should be raised in the same way.

This suddenly changed when Maia came home from an argument with Pablo. Both were 4 years old. They had been playing outside, and got into a typical children's argument. When Maia came home she was very upset. She told us that, in the heat of the argument, Pablo told her she was Black, and he was not. "How come I'm Black, and he's not, when he is darker than me?" Maia asked in confusion.

Suddenly we realized we had a problem. Actually we had several. The first was that Pablo freely used the Black label to put down a child. Additionally, how were we to answer Maia? And - most importantly to us - how were we to help Maia feel good about her physical features and identity?

So we did what good academics do - we sought out advice from experts; advice on how to raise healthy biracial children. And we found - none! What we did find was either a general acceptance that, of course, biracial children should be raised as Black, or the advice from many, that "we really don't know. Why don't you wait until we have some research, and then we can tell you." Well, obviously we couldn't wait!

So we discussed at length what each of us believed was important for our children - based partly on our education, but mostly on the way we were raised. And we found a local psychologist who had done some work with interracial families in a school in Kansas City. Beliefs from my background included a religion that taught all people are equal, regardless of nationality, culture or color; and multicultural personal experiences that include travel, working with Mayan Indians in the Highlands of Guatemala, and exposure to a variety of peoples and languages. Ruth's childhood experiences included growing up in Black communities, and attending White Catholic schools, where she was discriminated against for being Black. Her background also includes a very strong mother, and vital, educated, free thinking relatives.

When Maia was about 4, and our next daughter, Eirlys, was about 1, we came to the decision that our children would be raised with a combination of knowledge, appreciation and pride in Ruth's background and heritage, and in my background and heritage. They would not be raised as all White or all Black; neither were they to be raised as half White and half Black. We were going to raise our children as fully biracial - a new and different identity from a person with a single race identity. Just as a bicycle is a significantly different vehicle from a unicycle, so our children's identity is a combination of Black and White heritage. Biracial means both; it does not mean half and half.

As we explored raising our children as fully biracial we realized we had already started the process. When Maia was an infant we visited my parents and siblings in Pennsylvania. They live in a closed religious community with values, traditions and practices that are very much part of my heritage. In our days in Kansas City we often visited Ruth's mother and grandfather - a very handsome man who had been a Post Office worker. Our children were exposed to positive experiences with relative from Ruth's family and my family; neither family was perceived as better, more successful, more moral or more loved.

We have continued this process of supporting our children's total background and heritage, while also struggling with institutions, professionals and individuals who disagree with our approach. This book uses our experiences as an interracial family to provide advice, examples and ideas to other interracial families, teachers and other professionals committed to supporting the healthy development of all children in their programs, including biracial, multiracial and multiethnic children.

I feel this advice is sorely needed as the number of children of mixed heritage continue to increase, and as our schools, Head Start programs, little league teams and scout troops struggle to meet the needs of these children. As this population grows, there is more and more interest in this topic - through articles, seminars, talk shows and research papers.

Additionally adoptive parents are concerned about the best way to raise their biracial and multiethnic children. Because foreign adoption is becoming more difficult and because available White infants are very scarce, White American couples and singles are adopting minority children, including biracial and multiethnic children, in growing numbers. These parents face a unique series of challenges, including the best way to support their child's combined identity in a White home. They must also struggle against the current, negative attitude of many toward adoption of minority children by White parents.

Over the last 20-30 years of integration in this country, an emerging sense of pride and self-confidence on the part of interracial families has challenged many of the old myths, attitudes and practices. Interracial and multiethnic families are creating support groups, communicating to the public the reality of their families, and demanding multiracial categories on federal and census forms, to accurately reflect the heritage of their children. Over 60 education and advocacy groups now exist in this country; many of these groups publish authoritative and informational newsletters and provide internet sites; and several conferences and seminars are presented annually on issues of concern to interracial and interethnic families.

Interracial and interethnic families and their children come into contact with a variety of professionals: child care workers, adoption specialists, social workers, school psychologists and therapists, and teachers. Most of this contact is for normal profesional services; sometimes the family is in trouble, and needs intensive help. Unfortunately many of these professionals either know little about working with this population, or still believe in traditional notions about interracial and interethnic families and their children: interracial marriage is in some way abnormal and pathological; biracial and biethnic children have a very high probability of becoming dysfunctional; mixed-race children must be raised with the single identity of their parent of color; a combined identity will automatically cause confusion in a child, and children of mixed heritage - especially teenagers - are always left out of social groups and have no friends.

In the summer of 1996 our family spent a vacation in Wales. Our children were now much older: Maia, 19, Eirlys, 16, Kealan, 14, and RaEsa, 12. We stayed with my brother in an old farmhouse built in the 1700s. From the white painted farmhouse and old stone outbuildings, small fields and narrow, winding lanes radiate into the countryside. Buzzards and owls fly from the high roadside hedges. Cows, sheep and pigs are tended in the fields.

This farm in the border country between England and Wales is less than 100 miles from where I spent the first 12 years of my life. And it's a great reminder to me of my early years - rolling hills, winding footpaths; cattle, sheep, pigs, hens and sheep dogs; hard work and robust meals. Checking the cattle and sheep with my brother, with the keen sheep dog running obediently along, reminded me of my childhood days watching in awe as the trained dogs skillfully rounded up the sheep, several fields away. As a family we took trips further afield from the farm to view castles, traverse rivers, and follow footpaths across the fields, just like my family forays as a child into the beautiful English and Welsh countryside. And it exposed my children both to an important part of my heritage, and to much of their cultural roots. They also played English games with their cousins, and learned the joys of the farm: catching a squealing piglet, playing with the sheep dog, romping in the hay barn, and waking to a cock crowing.

My children know this is part of their background. They know the farm, the wild outdoors, and the history of castles, churches and walled cities, are all part of their heritage.

At one point on our vacation we rented a car and drove north to visit my mother's sister. A spry, opinionated lady in her 80s, Edna showed us where my mother grew up, talked about her family's experiences, and reminisced about my mother as a child. She was especially taken by one of my daughters - whom she said behaved just like my mother as a child. She gave the children a real feel for their grandmother's early life, and a sense of belonging to it.

My background is very much a part of their heritage. So is Ruth's background, which includes being denied access to the theaters and swimming pools as she grew up in Kansas City, the Trail of Tears, rural survival in Oklahoma, slavery, and Caribbean culture and traditions. It also includes a history of commitment to higher education, and an interest in women's rights and social equality. Recently Ruth has been researching her rich Chickasaw past - through birth certificates, names on Indian rolls, oral histories with distant relatives, and a visit to the Chickasaw Nation with the children. This has imbued in our children something of their Chickasaw roots, and their rich history.

Most importantly, my children know their background is a collection of cultures, histories and heritages that are not incompatible, don't have to be presented in opposition to each other, and can live together without contradictions and conflicts. They know you don't have to put down European culture to have pride in your Black heritage; they know their Black American heritage does not need to be viewed as inferior to European culture. And they don't have a need to create either an Afrocentric or Eurocentric viewpoint: its obvious and natural to them that both viewpoints can exist together, can compliment each other, and can be viewed as part of the whole. Our children are proud of their great, great grandfather who was one of the first Labor Members of Parliament in England, and another great, great grandfather who was a well-known medicine man.

This sense of acceptance of both Black and European heritage, this comfort of compatible but diverse heritages, and the notion that different backgrounds can work together to create a rich whole, rather than compete to create confusion, is what this book is about. It's an acceptance of who biracial and biethnic children are. It's an understanding of the reality of one's diverse heritage, while it rejects those who claim Black and White histories in America are too different and opposite to ever be united.

The purpose of this book is to help parents, teachers and other professionals develop a security, comfort and acceptance of children of mixed heritage, to challenge those who believe these children must reject their European heritage (or any part of their heritage), to insist multicultural education include and support a full biracial and multiethnic identity, and to provide specific ideas how people working with these children can support their healthy development.

This book provides information to interracial and interethnic parents, parents who have adopted children of mixed heritage, and teachers working with interracial families. And it provides support to interracial and interethnic families struggling to raise healthy children. These families include two parent interracial families, single parent (either the White or Black parent) families, blended families, and adoptive and foster homes. While much of the focus of the book is on biracial, Black/White children, its advice and issues are effective in working with all multiethnic and multiracial families whose parents crossed traditional U.S. categories to have children.

The information provided is also to help teachers and other professionals support this ever increasing segment of our child care and school population. This information is intended to help professionals understand the reality of these families, the struggles they go through, and the support and assistance they need in raising their children.

For parents, the book is intended to link them to a growing interracial community, to provide them with helpful hints, and to encourage them in their effort to raise healthy children.

Chapter one, *The Development of Healthy Biracial Children*, discusses two of the most difficult issues facing interracial families: the identity of their children, and how to handle the problem of a lack of a category for their children on census and OMB (the federal agency that determines categories on all the forms we have to fill out) forms and documents. (At the time of writing this book, the U.S. Census Subcommittee has recognized census categories that allow people to check more than one category. It is not clear how or if OMB will implement this new law for school programs).

Chapter two presents specific ideas for parents with children of mixed heritage - biological, adopted and blended. The ideas were specifically developed to help support these families and children. They suggest ways for parents to help in their child's racial identity development and to work with teachers and other professionals.

Adopted children have challenges different from biological children. Families who adopt these children also face unique issues. And families who invite multiracial and multiethnic children into their homes need information and support to help provide a warm, supportive home environment. Chapter three gives specific information to these families, and to child care programs and schools who serve adopted biracial and biethnic children - both domestic and foreign.

Chapter four addresses some general ideas to help programs working with multiracial and multiethnic families and their children become responsive to the needs of these families. The overall school and child care climate, training, resources, exploring diversity, and ideas for working closely with each interracial family, are all covered.

Chapter five covers interracial and interethnic families and biracial and multiethic children whose combined heritages are not Black/White. While Black/White interracial families are the most obvious example of crossing traditional racial lines in this country, to marry and have children, they are not the most common form of interracial and interethnic relationships. There are Asian, White relationships; Black and Native American marriages; White, Hispanic families; Chinese, Vietnamese marriages, and Asian, Black marriages. There also are marriages between representatives of groups that fit within traditional racial and ethnic categories, such as Mexican/Brazilian, and intertribal relationships (Papago, Navajo). And all of us are aware of inter-religious families. This chapter addresses issues faced by all these families.

The last chapter, chapter six, is titled, *Myths and Realities*. It explores many of the myths that exist about interracial and interethnic relationships, interracial families and children of mixed heritage (adopted and biological). Because of the taboo against interracial marriage in this country, many myths have developed to justify our dislike of these relationships and their offspring.

Principally this book is designed to support and assist parents and teachers sincerely and positively supporting the development of healthy, diverse, biracial and biethnic children. Its purpose also is to extend our concept of diversity and multicultural education to include the unique needs, histories and experiences of interracial and interethnic families and their children.

It is my hope that other interracial and interethnic families will gain a sense of pride and security from this book, and learn some specific ideas to help them raise healthy children. I also hope to positively affect the lives of these families and children by providing information and resources to programs and professionals: teachers, social workers, administrators, couselors and psychologists.

A word about language is needed. One of the results of any new human movement is to challenge exiting language and labels.

This is true of the current multiracial movement. Consequently different people use different terms. For this book I use biracial (two races), multiracial (three or more races), biethnic (two ethnic groups) and multiethnic (three or more ethnic groups). I also use interracial family (two races) and interethnic family (two ethnic groups). Clearly these terms are currently in dynamic flux, and will change over time, especially as the basic concepts of race and ethnicity in this country experience their own modifications.

To provide a gender balance, I will use masculine and feminine pronouns randomly for simplicity.

Chapter 1
The Development of Healthy Biracial Children

All parents of biracial children must decide on the racial identity of their child. Biological parents, parents of adopted children, and parents in blended homes that include a biracial child need to address this issues. While the question of the identity of a biracial child is most obvious when the child is of Black and White heritage, it is also important for all biracial and biethnic children, whatever the child's racial or ethnic heritage.

Not only is this issue one of the most critical issues interracial parents face, it is one that generates a great deal of debate in our society. The choice of the racial identity of a biracial child is made more difficult because many professionals working with biracial children either believe they must be raised as Black, or have no experience working with these children.

History of biracial identity in America

Ever since Blacks first came to this country we have had biracial (Black/White) children. Even earlier there were biracial children of White/Native American heritage. As other people of color (mostly men) were brought to this country to provide cheap labor for canals, railroads, gold mines and cotton mills, the number of biracial and biethnic children and adults increased. For a short period of time these children - and the adults they became - were generally accepted within the fabric of a new, egalitarian, free, democratic, multiethnic and multiracial society. But as the issue of slavery increased, so did the taboo against interracial marriage. So the children of these marriages were given the single identity of their minority parent.

Biracial children of Black/White heritage were identified as Black so they could remain the property of slave owners and not become free men and women (Frederick Douglass was a biracial slave). Further, to maintain the argument of the separation of the races, it was important to demonstrate Whites' superiority over Blacks, so interracial marriage became taboo. Many states passed laws strictly prohibiting interracial marriage. These laws stipulated that someone with any Black heritage - regardless of the amount - must have a Black identity - what is called today, the "one drop rule". The last of the laws prohibiting interracial marriage was declared unconstitutional by the Supreme Court in 1967; but the one drop rule is still accepted by many.

Most of the state laws prohibiting interracial marriage applied to all marriages between White Americans and Americans of color (Black, Native American, Filipino, Chinese, etc.). As a result biracial and biethnic children were raised with the racial identity of their parent of color. And these children were then raised in the minority community of their parent of color, unless they were European enough looking to pass as White. In the minority communities, as the prejudice of colorism and racial purity shifted, biracial and biethnic children were sometimes accepted (and even preferred), while at other times partially rejected for not being ethnic or dark enough.

The 1967 Supreme Court decision outlawing prohibition of interracial marriage, the 1954 Brown v. Board of Education decision eliminating the separate but equal doctrine, and the Civil Rights Movement of the 1960s, increased the integration of people of different races within schools, colleges and the work place. This naturally lead to an increase of interracial relationships and marriages, and biracial and biethnic children. And the new generation of interracial families was challenged to determine the best way to raise their children. Some of these families accepted the traditional practice of raising their biracial children as Black; others - like my family - challenged this practice. While we chose to raise our 4 children with a strong biracial identity, much of the advice provided in this book can also be used to raise healthy biracial and biethnic children whose parents take an different approach to their children's identity. All biracial and biethnic children, regardless of how they are raised, must feel positive about their total heritage, and be able to withstand identity confusion and harassment they will experience. Even if a child is raised as Black, or chooses a Black identity, (or the identity of their parent of color) she should not feel ashamed of her White heritage, or feel a sense of racial or ethnic confusion or insecurity.

The various approaches interracial parents have taken regarding their child's racial identity are: raising the child as Black; race is not an issue - my child is human; my child will make her own decision, when ready; and raising the child as fully biracial. For children whose parents of color are not Black, the child is raised with that parent's identity, or as biethnic. The common socially accepted approach is to raise a child with the identity of the parent of color; and, if the child's heritage includes a Black parent and a non-black parent of color, to raise the child as Black.

Raising a biracial child as Black

Viewing biracial children as having the single racial identity of their minority parent is the result of several factors. Today people often present this concept in the phase, "Society sees them as Black, so you must raise them as Black". Some parents and many professionals believe biracial children must be raised with the identity of their Black parent to develop a healthy and secure identity. They believe this because of the historical identity of biracial children, and because psychological theories of personality development stress a single race and a single racial community of support. (The field of psychology has not yet developed an approach to supporting children whose identity crosses over racial and ethnic groups. All current identity models stress identity development in relation to a single reference group - race or ethnicity.) In these times of heightened racial awareness and ethnic struggle, loyalty is another reason to raise biracial children as Black. Black parents who marry interracially will raise their children as Black to continue the struggle with their Black community. A White parent who attempts to raise her biracial child as biracial is often accused of wanting a biracial identity because of her dislike toward the Black race and its lack of status in this society.

Many believe biracial children are accepted by the Black community, but not by the White community. They believe this is especially true during the difficult period of adolescence, when friendships, dating, identity and a sense of self-worth are so critical, and when a child can so easily lose their way. It is believed a biracial adolescent who has Black friends, joins Black groups, and identifies with Black political issues, will successfully travel through the confusion of adolescence. Also, to be able to withstand the racism of our society, biracial children need to identify as Black, to learn Black survival skills and to have the support of a group that understands and has directly experienced racism, and who can help these children negotiate the trials of racism. Identifying with the Black struggle of harassment and oppression will enable biracial children to survive in a racist society.

Segregation by race, culture and ethnic group is still very common in this country. It becomes especially compelling during high school and college. Parents want their children to fit in. They don't want their children to be accused of rejecting their Black heritage, trying to be like Whites, and being better than their Black friends.

Raising biracial children as Black is supported by all aspects of our contemporary society. Radio talk shows, TV programs, newspaper and magazine articles, and social service professionals all strongly support this concept. Many of the Black children on the old Cosby TV Show are actually biracial; my daughters' role model is the biracial Olympic gymnast Betty Okino, whom the media call Black. Some of our children's friends initially call then Black.

Race is not an issue

Contemporary interracial families have their roots in the Civil Rights Movement of the 1960s. These parents sincerely believe that all humans are equal, and that the important aspects of humanity transcend race. They feel the sameness of people is greater than the difference between them. And they think using racial categories is an artificial system designed to keep people apart, and to enable some people to control others. So these parents of biracial children believe raising their children either with the label of her minority parent, or as biracial, perpetuates the racism of society. This idealist position about all people leads these interracial parents to raise their children as human above all else. They view their children as ambassadors of a new, raceless society. Thus they raise their biracial children without a racial label. And they believe good parenting styles that stress self-esteem development, responsibility, independence, and respect for all people will adequately prepare their children to succeed in this society, and change the society for the better.

My parents sincerely believe that God created all people as equals, and that racial and ethnic labels only function to separate and sort people. They have argued strongly with me against raising my children with a biracial label.

Many biracial children seem to support this approach. When our oldest was asked by a newspaper reporter doing a story about biracial teens, "What are you?" she shrugged her shoulders, and responded, "I'm a 13 year old girl." Other interracial parents have told us their children don't seem at all concerned about their racial identity.

My child will choose his identity

Another common approach to the identity issue is for parents to tell their children that they will raise them without a label, until the child is old enough to choose her own identity.

Parents who adopt this approach expose their children to a variety of people, activities, traditions, festivals and ideas. They talk openly with their children about various identity choices, about society's racism, and about a person's need for an identity. These parents believe their children will make an identity choice during adolescence. They also realize self identity is a developmental activity, and therefore their child might try on different identities, before finally settling on one. Finally they believe the ambiguity the child will experience during this process is a natural struggle that is not harmful to the child.

While parents who use this approach feel sincerely that their children have a right to select the identity they will live with for the rest of their lives, it could be argued these parents are avoiding making a difficult decision, and placing that responsibility on their children. They cannot be accused of being disloyal to the Black struggle; they will not feel guilty about denying their child exposure to his full cultural heritage. Further, we know all children - biracial and of single race - go through periods in their life where they define and redefine their identity. Yet most parents still believe it is important to raise their children with a clear sense of who they are. These children will eventually accept some of their parent's influence, while rejecting other parts of it.

A biracial identity

The focus of this book, as pointed out earlier, is on developing biracial and biethnic children with a healthy biracial and biethnic identity. My wife and I have raised our children to have a knowledge and pride in their total genetic, cultural and historical heritage. We believe our children are the product of both parents' backgrounds. And we know they have grown up in an environment that is uniquely different from that of a single race child. Further, we believe our children can develop a strong sense of this combined identity; and can then use this identity as a positive tool in the difficult task of healthy development in a narrow-minded, racist society. We believe that asking our children to deny one side of their parentage is both unfair to that parent and parent's extended family, and will cause the child a great amount of guilt. It will also limit the support and influence of the excluded family on the development of the child. Because raising children today is such a difficult task we believe biracial children need a strong sense of belonging. A biracial identity also provides a child with a label to use when people ask insensitive questions about, "Who are you anyway?" When people ask RaEsa (our youngest) what she is, her response is so automatic that even her gym-mates chime in with, "She's biracial." A biracial child raised with the pride and acceptance of all parts of her heritage will easily function with Black and White children, and will have a very wide tolerance for differences and diversity. She will not need to consider a child's racial label before she accepts him.

When Kealan, our son, first attended middle school, several Black children accused him of trying to be White, trying to be better than them. Because Kealan knows his heritage includes his White relatives, he was not ashamed of being accused of being White - because he knows he partly is!

Development of a healthy biracial identity

Biracial children follow the same developmental path as do single race children. And we know - and must never forget - that most of what a biracial child needs is the same as what all children need - love, acceptance, structure, nurturing and guidance. But we also know our children have unique challenges that must be addressed. The model for healthy development of biracial and biethnic children presented here is specific for children of Black (or parent of color) and White heritage. Many of the concepts, however, also work to a large extent for all biracial and biethnic children. This model comprises two developmental stages (early childhood and adolescence), and five environmental components.

Two time periods

There are two time periods in a child's life when issues of identity, self-worth, and self-esteem seem to be very important. These are the early childhood years (3 to 7) and adolescence. During these stages the child is going through a variety of important milestones in development. Establishing a positive, secure racial identity is one of these developmental tasks.

Early childhood time period. During the early childhood years children begin to explore who they are: gender, physical abilities, likes and dislikes, parents, siblings, schools they attend, people who become their friends, and their learning styles. The young child spends a lot of time and energy comparing herself to others, understanding how she fits into the family and school, and deciding about her identity. Young children are very self-centered. The whole world rotates around them. That's why the words "me" and "mine" are so common during this time. Not only are young children interested in who they are, but they are very honest in trying to find out about others. They will ask all sorts of questions, including questions about skin color, parents, age of parents, clothes, where their friends live, and "why so and so." They will compare their hair to that of a friend; they will stand next to each other to see who is the tallest; they will try out different clothes; and they will challenge each other to determine who can jump the farthest and run the quickest.

This is the time when most biracial children begin to ask

about their identity. Some of this curiosity seems to be triggered by questions asked of them by other children, such as, "Your daddy's white and your mother's black, so what are you?" and, "Are you black or are you white - I can't tell?" And some is triggered by prejudicial statements about the way they look. Not coincidentally these questions occur at the time many young children enter their first organized child care or school program. Many of these questions are very natural, since young children are trying to find out about their world, and how they fit into it. What we need to do is help the young biracial child find out who she is, respond to these questions, and help her feel good about being biracial. This is the age when self-identity starts, which is why it is so critical to support this exploration.

Biracial and biethnic children also need a verbal label to use to help them respond to all these questions. For the younger child the label 'brown' works well, because it is concrete and descriptive; at about age 4-5, she can use the terms 'biracial' and 'biethnic' effectively.

The single race child also needs help to understand biracial and biethnic children do not have to be only Black or White, but are a combination of both parents' physical traits. This is very difficult for young children to understand, because they think in absolute categories, and because they unquestionably accept what they hear from others.

At this age the biracial and biethnic child - and other minority children - often choose to play with White friends and White dolls. They also might express the wish they had blond hair, blue eyes, and White skin. An adopted minority child may say to her White mother that she wishes she looked like her. This is very normal, and should not produce concern on the part of parents or teachers. Recently I taught at a school in a small religious community, where the only non-White children were my children. One of my kindergarten children told her parents she wanted to be brown, just like my children. She even painted her face brown and painted pictures of brown people. She was very fascinated by my children, and - as young children do - she took a concrete approach to exploring that fascination. Young children want to be like their friends. They also love to experiment with the real world. Trying to look Black by a White child, and trying to look White by a Black child, is not a rejection of the child's racial identity: its an acceptance of the diversity they see around them, and a wish to explore that diversity.

There are two very important things to remember about identity development during these early years. First, young children are very primitive thinkers. They think in concrete terms, and they can only handle one piece of information at a time. For example, young children believe that what makes a person a woman are the clothes she wears and the work she does. A biracial child knows he is biracial because of his skin color, hair texture, and the skin color of both of his parents. He does not understand that his make-up is a combination of the Black race and the White race. A young Black child knows his skin color and the skin color of his parents make him Black. He does not know, however, that he is a member of the Black race. Secondly, at this age, children need an open, supportive and honest environment to explore their identity. This establishes a solid foundation for the more difficult process that occurs during adolescence. A parent of biracial and biethnic children cannot wait until the child is an adolescent before addressing the issue of racial identity. It must start during these early years. The chapters in this book on ideas and activities for the home and school provide specific suggestions to help children investigate and support this identity.

Adolescence. Adolescence is a very difficult time for all children in our society. It is a time when all parents become very concerned. Parents of biracial and biethnic children are often particularly fearful of this age. This is due to our natural concern about adolescent forays into non-academic activities, sex, music, fashion, cars, alcohol, etc., and because the public and professional view of biracial children often points to dysfunctional adolescents. Also many parents only become concerned about their child's identity, at this age. Adolescence is a time when a child naturally moves away from his parents and towards independence. Peer influence takes over from parental control and modeling.

Issues that affect biracial adolescents are similar to those that impact all adolescents. One of the best ways for parents to address adolescent issues is to first address these issues during the early years. Thus young children should be given some responsibilities and choices. To a degree they should also be held responsible for their actions and non-actions. If a biracial child enters adolescence with a strong self-concept, a clear understanding of her biracial or biethnic heritage, and a firm foundation in responding to people's questions, remarks and pressure, that child has a good chance of successfully completing adolescence.

Adolescents are very concerned about who they are, and how they fit in with other adolescents. Thus schools have lots of groups that segregate students by interest (choir, chess club, politics, French club), abilities (football, gymnastics, advanced classes, magnet programs), and race (African American Student Association, Hispanic Students, Native American Association). Further, adolescents - especially those who are not very secure with their own identities - exaggerate these differences to help boost their own sense of self-worth, and their own membership in the group. Athletes look down at 'nerds'; advanced students may make condescending remarks about students with disabilities; students in one racial or ethnic group might use dislike of those in another group to help define their identity and group solidarity; and students who identify their group membership by musical preference, usually disparage students with other preferences.

Informal groups at school also often follow these same grouping patterns and behaviors. When people argue that biracial and biethnic children must view themselves as Black or Hispanic or Native American, so that they have a group to belong to at school, they forget that most ability and interest groups at school are not race defined. It is incorrect to assume that an adolescent must select a single racial identity in order to develop a sense of belonging. Also, these single race and ethnicity student groups often do not accept a student of mixed parentage unless that student totally rejects the part of their background not represented by the group. My oldest daughter found a school identity group based on her love of gymnastics; Eirlys, our second child, has friends defined by the International Baccalaureate Program and gymnastics; Kealan's groups seem to be based on a choice of music and soccer.

Adolescents also have social groups outside of school. These include church youth groups, interest groups (soccer, scouts, gymnastics, nature groups), service groups and neighborhood friends. These groups often complement what is available at school, and will rarely be race specific.

Interracial parents should find groups for their children (in and out of school) that expose them to children from a variety of racial and ethnic backgrounds, and allow them to feel comfortable around diversity. While it is important that some of the children they interact with are from interracial and interethnic families, it is most important that they learn to enjoy cultural, racial and ethnic diversity. Unfortunately some groups in and out of school are concerned with racial and ethnic purity. Clearly these groups are not good places for biracial and biethnic children to attend. Since few schools have groups specifically for biracial or biethnic children, these children should select groups based on skills and interests, or advocate for a mixed heritage student support group.

Environmental factors

A child's successful passage through childhood depends on support from the environment - institutions, churches, friends, helping professionals, parents, teachers, and peers. While all experiences effect the child's total development, there are 5 general environmental influences that directly impact biracial and biethnic children. These are: family, community, majority influence, minority influence, and the effects of prejudice. For children whose parents are both members of different minority groups, the relationship between these groups will impact the child's development.

Family. Clearly the family is the most important influence on developing children. This is especially true when the child is young. The healthy family establishes the child's moral code, and sets the stage for prejudice or tolerance. A healthy family also gives the young child responsibilities and freedoms that create independence and self-assurance. If the family does a good job of teaching their child the fundamentals of justice, self respect, independence and racial pride, when the child moves away from family security and comes under the influence of peers, she will have a good foundation to withstand negative peer pressure, including racism and harassment.

By family I mean a secure social unit with parents, extended family, and siblings. This includes single parent homes, blended families, and foster and adoptive families.

Many interracial and interethnic parents realize how important they are in the healthy development of their children. They are very concerned with their children's education, developing an appreciation for all people, and creating biracial and biethnic pride in their children. These parents buy their children multiracial materials, expose them to children from a variety of backgrounds, and provide a healthy family environment.

It is important for parents to spend as much time as possible with their children when they are young. It is not so important what parents do. Our family visited 1850 replica villages, wildlife sanctuaries, museums and festivals. We visited New Mexico and Pennsylvania to visit friends and family. I often took one of my children with me on business trips to Washington, D.C., and other cities. Time at home was spent gardening, playing games, practicing gymnastics and soccer, and reading.

The family establishes the foundation for the child's sense of pride in her identity and heritage. The family also teaches the child how to respond to questions about her identity, and how to feel good about being different.

Community. As children grow older the community beyond home has greater influence. This community includes child care, Head Start, school, school groups (choir, gymnastics, athletics, etc.), out-of-school groups (soccer, scouts), peer groups, church and interracial support groups.

It is important that interracial parents become advocates for their children in these community groups. This is difficult, because many parents are reluctant to do things that will bring attention to their children. When I told a principal that our two oldest girls were neither Black nor White, but biracial, the principal told his teachers that I was "uptight" about my children's identities. Many interracial and interethnic parents feel their child are normal - and should be treated that way.

Unfortunately, other people do not see our children as normal, and most community groups our children join will view them at best as a curiosity, and at worst, negatively. Whether we like it or not, we must be concerned about the impact of these groups on our children. Children's self esteem is largely developed by the way important people in their lives respond to them. If these responses are positive, the child will develop a positive self esteem.

There are several things we can do. Some of these will be discussed in other chapters (schools, child care, support groups, home activities, and peers). Selecting an integrated neighborhood in which to live, joining an interracial support group, and participating in festivals, ethnic celebrations and community groups, all provide positive experiences for young biracial and biethnic children. Our family has moved because of the negative impact of the community. We moved from Kansas City to Denver; and we also moved within Denver, to find a supportive neighborhood and appropriate schools. There is no question certain cities and neighborhoods are better places to live than others for interracial families. Each family must determine - through personal contacts and word of mouth - the best place to live.

As I have already stated, during the adolescent stage peer groups have tremendous impact on all children. So the schools families choose for their children are very important, as are in-school and out-of-school groups they join.

Majority Influence. Biracial and biethnic children must be able to integrate both sides of their heritage. This is done in a variety of ways, including contact with both sides of the family, developing pride in both family trees, and many open family discussions. This is possible, especially if the child is not viewed as half Black and half White, (or half one minority heritage and half another) or all Black; (or all the ethnic group of the parent of color), but rather viewed as an integrated whole: biracial or biethnic. All children are products of the values and backgrounds of both their parents, and both sets of extended families. This involves integrating several points of view by the child. For biracial - Black/White children - this means integrating majority and minority cultures. For biethnic children with no White heritage, there is still often a more socially preferred group and a less socially preferred group represented in their heritage.

The majority group in this country is obviously White. And, while this group is comprised of religious, national and ethnic diversity, it tends to hold a dominant position in many areas: popular culture - TV, radio, films, magazine covers; academic culture - books, pictures, text book content; and political and economic power. Most Whites in this country view racism and prejudice as functions of individual attitude, not as institutional or systemic. They believe anyone in this country can succeed, if they work hard enough; and some Whites view minorities in stereotypical (but not necessarily negative) ways. Our son, Kealan, is an avid and aggressive soccer player. He is the only non-White member of his soccer team. Because of his competitive nature and minority status, he is called for many more fouls than any other member of the team. Parents of other team members have told me his athletic ability is due to his Black heritage.

To succeed in this country everyone must learn to function effectively within the dominant culture. But this does not mean a minority child should reject his heritage, or believe he is somehow inferior. A biracial or biethnic child must never try to hide his minority heritage to succeed. This is particularly tempting for those biracial and biethnic children who look European.

Minority Influence. Most Americans will initially view the biracial child as a minority. This may be the same race or ethnicity as her parent of color, or it might be a mistaken identity, based on the child's physical appearance. My oldest daughter is frequently assumed to be Hispanic or Asian- Indian. My second daughter was photographed by tourists when we visited my friend at the Taos Pueblo, because she looks Native American. The biracial and biethnic child must feel comfortable and attached to her minority heritage.

While Blacks in this country are becoming more and more diverse - economically, politically, and religiously - many view themselves more as a single group than Whites view their group. This is particularly true around issues of political solidarity, history of past struggles, and efforts to improve the status of Blacks in American economic and political society. This attitude is often evident in Black students on college campuses, and those involved in community activities. The sense of group solidarity and unity is supported by the current trends of racial pride, activism, and sometimes a move toward segregation.Until very recently biracial children and adults were only accepted in communities of color. Many minorities believe this entitles them to demand that contemporary interracial families identify with and support the Black community. This attitude is also behind the insistence by some Blacks that biracial individuals view themselves as exclusively Black. This is also true of many biethnic individuals and their communities of color.

Children of mixed heritage need to understand why many minorities are uneasy about their choice of a biracial or biethnic identity, and why there is opposition by some in communities of color to their families' insistence that the biracial and biethnic child is neither Black or White, Hispanic or Asian. Older minorities who were raised in a society where children of mixed heritage had no choice but to identify with their parent of color, believe this is still the reality, and that biracial and biethnic children who try to proudly embrace their total heritage will become disappointed and hurt.

Group dislike. Biracial and biethnic children experience prejudice from a variety of sources, and in a variety of ways. Initial comments - like those between Maia and Pablo - will be caused more from misunderstanding than outright prejudice. Later - during adolescence - most biracial and biethnic children receive harassment from both minority and White peers. They may also receive a lack of sensitivity from professionals: teachers, counselors, psychologists, administrators and social workers.

Interracial and interethnic families must help their children handle these antagonisms. Of most importance is providing a secure, nurturing home where the child can return for security and understanding. Many of the discussions at our family dinner table are about prejudice, discrimination, and why so many people need to put others down. We also discuss the need in this country for institutions, including the government and schools, to put everyone into little racial boxes. And we intervene with our children's teachers and schools if discriminatory behavior is present. If it continues we remove our child. Biracial and biethnic children need to know their parents will intervene, if needed.

Many interracial families respond to group hatred by retreating into a very small family world (adoptive families often do the same thing). They stay home a lot, and only socialize with other interracial families and supportive relatives. This is very dangerous. Interracial and interethnic families should explore their community, the country and the world. They should advocate for their children and protest injustices against their families and children. We must believe in our families and children, and show our children that these beliefs cause us to take positive action.

Conclusion

Biracial and biethnic children can be raised to become healthy individuals. Parents must understand the unique needs of their children, and provide for these needs. Critical to this healthy development is the racial identity they are raised with, and supportive environments at home and school. Children raised from the early years with a pride and appreciation of their total heritage have the best chance of developing into secure adults.

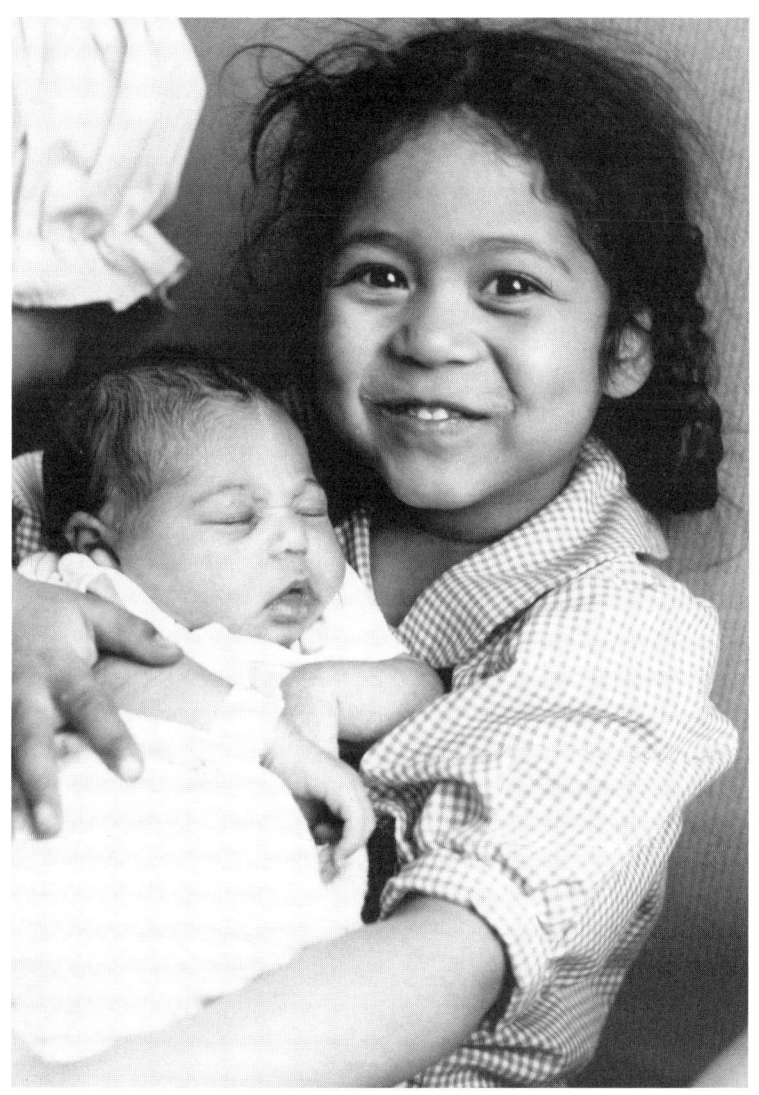

Table of Age-Related Issues for Interacial and Interethnic Families

	Environment (Home & School)	Working with Professionals/Teachers
Pre-marriage	Expose each other to both of your environments - home, neighborhoods, favorite eating places, etc. Learn to feel comfortable in each other's environment	Openly discuss interracial/interethnic marriage. Don't allow professionals to interject subjective arguments. Deal realistically with possible consequences, including loss of friends and relatives.
Marriage	Many home issues are the same as all newly married: affordable, size, location, neighborhood. Try to live in an integrated neighborhood, one that supports both of you.	If marriage conflict requires counseling/therapy, don't let race become a major issue. Look at interpersonal problems, relatives, etc. Isolate racial issues from other issues.
Birth and infertility. 0-2 year old child (biological/ adopted)	Mirrors to view self. Make house child-safe. Get quality child care. Evaluate child care for support of multiracial children. Books, dolls, pictures, and materials must reflect all races.	Biracial babies (Black/White) may be smaller than White babies and very light. Make sure professionals respond to your child as an individual, not a stereotyped category. Many professionals make race-based assumptions
2-5 year old child (biological/ adopted)	Mirrors to view self. Multiracial dolls, books, posters, puzzles. If in child care, try to find one with caregivers with a variety of racial backgrounds - also children. Look for mixed race friends for children, if possible.	Let professionals know your child is biracial or biethnic. If adopted, also insist professionals respond to child's mixed identity. Don't let professionals assume problems are automatically caused by adopted/biracial status.
5-11 year old child (biological/ adopted)	School should have staff and students with various racial backgrounds. Have art and books around the home and school that reflect various peoples and country of origin of adopted child.	Monitor professionals' support, both of biracial and biethnic identity and adoptive status. Remove child if this is not occurring. Educate teachers and others.
Adolescence/ dating	Try to have child attend an integrated school, and choose clubs and groups based on interest, not ethnic makeup. Encourage membership in groups away from school that compliment the school environment.	If child needs therapy or is in counseling, don't assume a professional of color is necessarily supportive of biracial and biethnic identity. If a therapist feels child is denying his minority status, examine carefully.
Young adult	At this time, your child will probably be on her own. Your involvement will be very limited - listening, advice, etc.	If the young adult seeks psychological help, don't allow the professional to blame you, the parent, for her problems, especially in the area of identity.

Physical Care of Child	Relatives
Find out what's important to your companion, based on his/her cultural and family background.	Be open with relatives. Try not to avoid or dismiss relatives. Even if they disapprove, they are your relatives, and will not go away. Try to develop a relationship. Your children need them.
Learn about the care methods used by the culture of your spouse or the minority side of adopted child's background.	Invite all - even those who have expressed objection. Try not to shut the door on those who object - leave it open.
Learn how to care for child's hair. Also skin, if it tends to get dry or flaky. Know about dark marks that some minority children get that are mistaken for bruises (abuse).	Many reluctant grandparents fall for their new grandchildren. Expose children often to both sets of grandparents and uncles/aunts. Don't let past disagreements get in the way.
Learn various hair styles for your child's hair. Understand your children can get sunburn. Find clothes that look good with their skin color.	Continue as much exposure as possible. Request gifts that represent both cultures, races. Emphasize the genetic and individual characteristics of both sets of grandparents in children. Don't devalue either background.
Help with hair and dry skin. Help with selecting complementary clothes. Help child to select fashion style unique to herself.	As much exposure as possible, have relatives talk to your children about their heritage and what's important to them. See if relatives can help with children's research projects, including through E mail.
Help with appropriate hair styles, fashion choices, and makeup. Address dry skin, if a problem. Provide oils for dry hair. Find a barber who can cut and style your child's hair.	Time visiting various relatives will give your child a good sense of diversity. Regular correspondence is also helpful.
Stress the need for self-respect, especially in the area of sex. Also discuss the negative effect of drugs.	Support the young adult's contact with relatives she has grown to trust and enjoy. This is healthy.

21

Information compiled with imput from Pat Edwards and the Interracial Family Circle, Washington, DC.

	Talking with Spouse & Children	Identity / Support
Pre-marriage	Discuss society's and relatives' response to your possible marriage. Discuss how you will handle discrimination. Talk about how you will raise your children.	Support each other's ethnic, racial and cultural background. Feel proud of who you are. Don't give up your background to fit that of your spouse. Don't feel guilty. Start developing your own unique culture.
Marriage	Don't let society's opposition either stop you or force you to do something out of stubbornness. Know there are many successful interracial marriages.	Discuss your identity as an interacial couple and how people respond. Feel good about this collective identity. Join a support group of other interacial couples. Read material.
Birth and infertility. 0-2 year old child (biological/ adopted)	Discuss possible religious conflicts (example baptism); also how to respond to insensitive comments from strangers. How do you tell them your child is adopted or biracial? Talk about it.	Be proud of your child's total identity, don't hide any of it. Be comfortable talking to others about it. Expose children to other adopted and biracial children.
2-5 year old child (biological/ adopted)	Talk to children about similarities and differences, how we get physical characteristics and other traits from both sides of the family. Respond to any questions of your children.	This is the usual time when children are curious about hair texture, eye shape, skin color, etc. Talk openly about being proud to be different and to have a mixed heritage.
5-11 year old child (biological/ adopted)	Be open to your children about their adoptive status, and anything you know about their birth parents. Talk about the naturalness of biracial and biethnic children - both adopted and biological.	Children this age need labels and words to help them. Biracial, brown, adopted all help. Help them articulate their identity and feel good about it.
Adolescence/ dating	Talk about dating, and how you experienced it as a child. Help child view people as individuals, not categories. Help them select dates that have similar interests, etc.	Child's identity will be challenged by Black students, White students, and teachers. Help child educate these people and articulate who they are! Help child understand she does not have to justify who she is, or her racial choice.
Young adult	The young adult will rarely seek your advice. When she does, assure her of your support, and the rightness of her identity choice.	Identity challenge should be viewed as a problem of the challenger, not your son. Help him see he does not have to prove who he is.

Materials (books, etc.)	Racial Categories
Read books about interracial/ interethnic marriage (for example, *Mixed Blood*, by P. Spickard). Read articles - academic and in the popular press. Contact web sites.	Discuss with each other the question of your own racial/ethnic identity and the label you use to represent that identity. If your heritage includes Native American, Black and Asian, how do you define and label yourself?
Find out what each of you enjoy, and what you can learn from each other - music, dance, art, literature - without being phoney.	Discuss the question of the official label for your birth or adoptive child. What are your choices? Will you accept one of the labels provided by the government, or refuse to select from the limited government choices?
Read books about interracial families. Listen to lullabies from various cultures, such as Paul Robeson's, "My Curly Headed Baby." Read articles and books about biracial children and minority children.	Many states will request identity of child for birth certificate. Also, if you take out SS card at this time, it also asks for this. Insist your child is biracial or biethnic. The agency cannot make you fill out Black or White.
Children's books of interracial families and adoption. Dolls of various races. Puzzles, posters, etc. that show adoptive and interracial families. Avoid materials that break down world into distinctive races and groups.	Preschools, Head Starts, child care programs, etc. all request racial category of your child. Insist on biracial. If they refuse, check "other," or refuse to fill out, or do what both of you are comfortable with.
Artifacts, pictures, calendars, books, brochures, etc. of a variety of cultural groups: Native American, West Indian, African, etc. Materials of smaller groups: Guatemalan Indians, Polish, Kenyan. Avoid tribalism, etc.	During this age, children have to fill out their own categories. Discuss with your biracial child - biological or adopted - what categories to use and what to do if officials make it difficult.
Provide reading books on adoption, biracial identity, racism, and interracial families. Provide material about heroes who are biracial or adopted. Show children TV programs and articles in popular press that address adoption and interracial people.	Discuss openly the category your child believes they belong to - or if they dislike the whole notion. Can your child force a change in his schools? Can she talk to the press. Can she develop a multiracial student group?
Books about any successful person who has challenged society, especially autobiogra- phies. For example, Paul Robeson, James Early Jones, Maria Tallchief, Betty Okino, Dan O'Brian.	At this time your child probably will have selected a category that meets her needs. Support that choice. Some children this age feel the government has no right to label them.

Chapter 2
Ideas and Activities for Home

Introduction

The unique needs of biracial and biethnic children require parents to provide a deliberate approach to raising their children. In this chapter I offer ideas for interracial and interethnic parents to raise healthy children. It is, of course, understood that good child rearing advice given to parents of single race children apply here. I am just providing additional advice specific to families raising mixed-race children. In chapter four approaches used by early childhood programs and schools to assist in this healthy development will also be discussed.

There are important issues to be faced by interracial and interethnic couples even before the birth of their first child. Because it is so critical biracial and biethnic children have contact with both sides of their heritage, every effort must be made to have each side of the family support the marriage. This careful consideration of extended family support should also be made by a family contemplating adopting a biracial or biethnic child. In both cases it is important not to let society's racism get in the way of understanding how much easier it is to raise mixed-race children with support and love from the entire extended family. While some relatives change once the child is been born or adopted, some do not. Do all you can to win over your relatives before children become part of the family.

Spend time finding out about each other, about each other's backgrounds, and each other's likes and dislikes. While doing so, it is critical each partner honor and respect his and her own backgrounds. Share each other's interests and expectations. Ruth and I discovered we had a lot in common: I grew up in England, while Ruth always enjoyed English history and literature; we both were raised in strict religious homes and schools; we both love to travel and enjoy children, and we both enjoy folkdancing and are concerned with social issues.

Infancy

It's good to expose your child to diversity from the onset. Clearly an infant is not concerned with race and skin color, although infants can tell the physical difference. But as she learns about the physical world around her, it's important she learn that the world is full of different people and objects. If you are on good terms with your relatives, have them help you care for your infant. All of my children experienced my parents' religious community life when they were young. They were held by aunts and uncles, loved the community singing, and experienced the communal child care. Maia was lucky enough to meet one of my English grandmothers and one of my English grandfathers. All of our children have had ongoing contact with parts of Ruth's family, although her mother died when Maia was a baby. Maia and Eirlys also visited Ruth's grandfather on several occasions before his death.

Take your infant to community activities where she can be exposed to a variety of people; if you use an infant program, try to find one with a variety of caregivers (Black, White, Hispanic, Asian, multiracial and multiethnic), and a variety of infants. When Eirlys (my second child) was an infant, one of her caregivers was a Sikh living in a nearby ashram.

Clearly an infant bonds easily and quickly to her mother. In an interracial family the mother will be either Black or White; in an adoptive family, almost always White; and in an interethenic family, any race or ethnicity. I believe the child needs to be exposed to adults from both sides of his background early on. The easiest way for this to occur in interracial and interethnic families is for the father to become actively involved in raising his children at infancy. It is also crucial for the father to bond early with his child - especially if the father is not living with the child.

For the adoptive family and one-parent home, the task of exposing the child to both backgrounds is more difficult. An effort should be made for the child to have frequent contact with adults who represent the side of the child's identity not represented by his parents or parent. This can be achieved through friends, child care arrangements, and contact with relatives of the missing parent. Many parents of adopted biracial and biethnic children achieve this goal by joining interracial or multiracial support groups; or by creating their own. Some adoption agencies also provide support groups where transracial adoptive families can meet, socialize, support each other and receive expert advice and training.

The home

As your child gets older she continues to need an environment that reflects all sides of her identity. Materials in the home should reflect White, minority, biracial, and biethnic people and families. Calendars, artwork, magazines, family photos, books, puzzles, coloring books, posters, records, music tapes, and ethnic newspapers, along with personal artifacts, can help establish a multicultural environment. Include artwork and pictures that reflect the range of human diversity beyond that of your family. When displaying photos of your extended family make sure they are not displayed by race. Mix them up. In our home we have pictures of our family and relatives, drawings of children by a friend, black/white photographs of Guatemalan Indians I took during my stay in the Highlands of Guatemala, and recent pictures of my trip to Brazil.

Young children love to look at themselves in the mirror - to discover who they are, what they look like, and how they compare to others. This behavior also teaches them to feel good about themselves. Provide a full length mirror. Also provide dolls of various ethnic backgrounds, early reading books about interracial and interethnic families, multi-colored crayons and paints (Lakeshore and Crayola have these available), and a variety of music and lullabies. Hair brushes, combs, colorful ribbons and barrettes etc., will encourage the biracial girl to play with her hair and feel good about its color and texture.

There are some beautiful minority dolls on the market (for example, Discovery Toys) - but very few biracial and biethnic dolls; also there are a few books and puzzles that reflect biracial and biethnic themes. There are a variety of books for children with stories and pictures of people of different races. Again, however, there are only a few books about mixed race families and children. However, the number and range of these books is slowly increasing. Read to your children books about the minority and multiracial heroes Paul Robeson, Frederick Douglass, Booker T. Washington, James Audubon, Althea Gibson, Marion Anderson, Jesse Owens, Wilma Rudolph, Maria Tallchief, Betty Okino, Dan O'Brien, and others.

Our family made Paul Robeson's lullaby, "My Curly Headed Baby" the signature tune for our 4 curly headed infants. We often listened to recordings of Paul Robeson singing this wonderful song, and sang it to each of our children at night time. We also collect the Lladro collection of porcelain Black dolls, when we can afford to.

From my European background we have adopted the tradition of Saint Nicholas visiting every night from December 6 to December 24, leaving little gifts in our children's shoes. And we have developed over the years a tradition of inviting friends for a tree trimming party a few days before Christmas. Every family should find unique ways to celebrate their family's unique history and heritage.

Relatives

As I have already stated, it is very important to expose your children to both sides of your family. An African proverb states that a marriage is a union between two families. In this racist society it is often difficult to do this. But the child of mixed heritage must have real experiences with people from her minority and White heritage. If your parents - on either side of the family - refuse contact with you and your child, make contact with great grandparents, uncles and aunts, or distant relatives. Make every attempt to have a positive relationship with someone from both parents' side of the family, and try not to let wounds from rejection of a relative prevent them from contact with your children. This contact is very important for the healthy development of your child.

Our family travel almost every year to visit my parents and siblings in Pennsylvania. We also lived in their religious community for a year. When Ruth's mother lived in Kansas City, we visited often before she died. We have also stayed in contact with Ruth's only brother, who now also lives in Denver. We now have regular contact with him and his family. And, as I have already discussed, we have also visited my brother's farm in S. Wales. Never close the door completely with a parent, for the sake of your child. Many interracial and interethnic couples report that once hostile grandparents become totally converted with the arrival of a cute grandchild. Allow them to change their minds.

Most single parents of biracial children are White women. It is very important these parents try to stay in contact with the family and friends of their child's father. The mother should also try to maintain friends in the Black community, live in an integrated neighborhood, and join an interracial advocacy/support group. The White mother of a biracial child cannot allow herself to believe her marriage didn't work because of racism. She cannot now choose, because of her failed relationship, to segregate herself from all Black people. Part of her child's heritage is Black, and she must help her child feel good about his Black heritage. This contact needs to occur through regular, informal interactions. A White single parent of a biethnic child has the same challenges to overcome.

White adoptive parents also need to continue to expose their biracial and biethnic children to minority adults and children. Joining a support/advocacy group - or creating your own - is one way to achieve this; another is to have your child attend an integrated child care program and school.

Creating a family tree - with photographs, drawings and other family treasures - is a great way to help the young child learn about his rich heritage. Family customs and traditions - of both families - should be practiced and enjoyed. A family book can be made; a calendar using family portraits works well; family photo albums should be collected.

Open discussion

At about age 3-4 years of age, biracial children ask questions about their physical appearance, about comments made by their peers, and inconsistencies they see in the world around them. They might ask, "Am I Black like you mummy, or White like my daddy?" They might say, "Johnny said I am Black, and he doesn't want to play with me because I'm Black." Or, "My teacher told the other children that I'm Black like Tommy - but I'm brown, aren't I?"

Neighborhood children, children in the local daycare or school, and people at shopping centers, museums and galleries, often either make insensitive comments, ask awkward questions, or just stare. When our children were young an elderly woman saw Ruth with them in a Safeway store, came up to her and said, "It's so nice you adopted Vietnamese orphans." When my boss saw a photo of Eirlys in my office he said he was surprised I had adopted a Native American child.

Openly respond to your child's questions. "Your mother is Black, and father is White - so you're brown, just like coffee that is mixed with milk." "People stare at interracial and interethnic families because they are not used to them. And some people are uncomfortable with our families." "Tell your friends you are brown because your daddy is White and your mummy is Black."Also talk to your children about how society rarely shows interracial and interethnic families. Many high profile minorities (on TV, in sports) are, in fact, biracial or biethnic. Respond to your children at their level - and within the context of their questions. A lecture or historical explanation is not needed. Most importantly, provide an environment where your child can openly discuss the experiences he has at daycare, school and in the neighborhood, and the images he see in books, magazines and on TV.

Do not isolate yourself

A critical task for the healthy development of all young children is to be able to move from the security of their home to the wider world of the neighborhood and school. The only way for this to occur is for parents to assist and support this natural process of development. Parents must support the child's experimentation and risk-taking. They need to provide a home where children can return to talk about their experiences and gain new confidence.

This concept is critical for the interracial and interethnic family to understand. You cannot totally protect your child from society's insensitivity and injustice. An adoptive parent has the same challenges. Some adoptive families make the mistake of exposing their children only to other adoptive families.

Parents who have mixed-race children - biological or adopted - challenge some deep seated values of our society - racism, the need for conformity, and the desire to categorize. It is critical parents of biracial and biethnic children let their children know by word and behavior that they are proud of their child's identity and appearance, and will support their experiences in the world beyond home.

This does not mean that interracial parents should not make decisions for their family based on society's racist response to their family. As I have said, some parts of the country are better places for mixed-race families to live in than others, certain communities and neighborhoods are more accepting than others; and some schools, teachers and childcare programs are not good places for our children. For the health of your children these decisions must be made.

Interest in physical features

All young children are very curious about what makes them who they are (skin color, height, running ability, gender, parents, and where they live), and children like to experiment to learn to feel comfortable with themselves (boys dress-up as girls, girls paint their faces like adults). They are learning about themselves by comparing and contrasting their physical characteristics with their peers, their siblings, images they see in the media, and their parents. It is how they come to terms with the physical part of their identity. Because of this interest in their physical characteristics and abilities, young biracial and biethnic children are very curious about why their skin color, hair texture, eye color, and eye shape, are different from their friends. "Am I like daddy or mummy?" And, "Why can't my hair look like yours?" Your child's single race friends are equally curious about your children. Talk to your child about how all children's physical characteristics and abilities come from a combination of their parent's characteristics and abilities. Don't say, "You can't be White," when your child expresses that wish; don't say "Don't play with the White dolls". For biracial and biethnic children, White adults and children dominate their out-ward experiences - TV, magazines, childcare, neighborhood, etc.

So they naturally want to play with what they see around them. They also have to find out - through direct experience (young children do everything through direct experience) how they are like their friends, and how they are different.

Hair and skin care

Biracial and biethnic children have a range of hair types, from straight to curly and frizzy. Many biracial children start out with straight hair, which turns frizzy as they grow older. And the color of biracial children's hair can be the range of all hair colors, including red and blond. Biracial children's frizzy and/or curly hair requires totally different care from straight hair. Skin care of biracial children is also different, and requires lots of moisture, especially in dry climates. If the mother in the family is Black, then she probably will know how to address these needs. Black men may not know how to care for the hair of their biracial daughters, because, until recently, men in our society did not take care of girls. The family may have to get help from Black relatives or advice books. As the children get older the issue of hair and skin care become more complex.

Parents whose children have frizzy hair will also have to seek out barbers who have experience cutting 'Black' hair. We have found this to be a tricky task. Many stores that cater to Whites do not know how to cut and care for our children's hair. And boys' hair needs are very different from those of girls. However, don't automatically assume a barber in a store serving Black customers necessarily knows what you want either. Careful research on your part is needed. And be careful about using the term 'good hair' and 'bad hair'. Many in the Black community use these terms to discriminate non-kinky, straight hair, from kinky, curly hair. Also realize that not all Whites carry genes just for straight hair. Hair is a very important part of a child's self-esteem: children must find ways to explore their hair and learn different ways to take care of it. My sisters have very thick, curly hair; my hair has been un-wieldy since I was a child. So we talk about the thick, curly hair our children got from my side of the family, along with the hair genes from Ruth's heritage.

Be care about conflicts that might arise out of different approaches to your children's hair and clothes, because of the different backgrounds and expectations of each parent. Parents, regardless of their backgrounds, bring to the family values, atti-tudes and opinions based on the way they were raised. These are neither right nor wrong, but must be respected and resolved. Resolve these disagreements the way all families resolve conflicts. All parents have to openly discuss their expectations and possible difference about discipline, TV, religion, clothes, spending money, work around the house, school work, and gender differences. Many Black girls pierce their ears at a much earlier age than their White counterparts, and use lots of colorful ribbons, barrettes and braids in their hair. It is nice if traditions from one or both sides of the family can be incorporated in these decisions. My three girls used the ribbons and barrettes from their Black heritage but often had their long hair in two braids, from my European background.

All these decisions, however, must be negotiable. It's not appropriate to say, "Well, all Blacks do their hair this way," or, "Everyone knows this is the good way to treat Black hair."

Neighborhood

An interracial family automatically integrates a neighbor-hood! But, as I have said earlier, a more equally integrated neigh-borhood is almost a must for any interracial or interethnic family (biological, adoptive, foster and blended). I have found that univer-sity communities are highly integrated, with minority families, international families and interracial families. Schools and childcare programs in these communities are also integrated. In a large city, the areas around these universities are often good places to live.

Interracial and interethnic families that live in segregated neighborhoods should take their children to playgrounds that serve a wide variety of families. Also expose your young child to a variety of cultures through visits to museums and libraries, attending ethnic festivals, dance presentations, fashion shows and art galleries. It's not so much that he needs exposure to White and minority culture; rather exposure to the richness of the people who make up this country will help him feel good about his cultural richness. He will also learn to enjoy and understand differences.

Dutch festivals, Greek dances, African American cultural celebrations, Native American Pow Wows, and countries of the world festivals, can all be enjoyed by the family. Each community has its own unique festivals and celebrations. You might also travel to other cultural activities.

For a while in Kansas City I danced with a Mexican folkloric dance group, so we attended lots of Hispanic festivals. Later I performed Morris (English) dances and Welsh dances, so we attended Celtic and English folk festivals in the mountain communities of Colorado. Other folk festivals also attracted out attention.

One year we visited a good friend of mine in Taos, New Mexico. This friend - Sonny - is a Pueblo Indian who participates in the religious and seasonal ceremonial dances. We watched the ceremony in the large communal plaza, and then visited with the women in their 500 year old adobe homes as they prepared the food for the male participants.

Day care and school

Organized children's programs are often the place where a child of mixed heritage first experience questions, comments and sometimes insults about her identity. So it is very important for a parent to have a good relationship with the child care center or school. Children cared for in a home setting (home based child care) are also exposed to these same questions and prejudices. The first person we approached to care for our oldest daughter told us she would not care for her, because she had once had a bad experience with an interracial family.

Before you enroll your child, examine whether the program will support your child's total identity. Look at the ethnic make up of the staff and children attending the center. What about the curriculum materials and posters on the walls? Are there Black, Asian and Hispanic dolls? Are there posters of a variety of people, families and children? Look at the children's books, puzzles and workbooks. Also examine advertising materials and parent communication information for examples of a multicultural approach.

There is a good range of multicultural materials available for child care centers and schools (although almost no interracial and books, posters, dolls). Many educational programs are also involved in a national movement to create anti-bias curricula and environments. This is an effort to support the cultural heritage of every child in the child care and school program. Unfortunately some of these efforts - especially in public schools - ignore interracial and interethnic families and their children. Or they just lump them in with the cultural group of their minority parent. This can cause problems for biracial and biethnic children. The son of a friend of mine was asked by his teacher to research the life of a favorite relative, and bring pictures of that relative to the class. This biracial child collected information about his White/Carib grandfather, who had been an important politician of his day. The teacher rejected the boy's contribution, because the grandfather was not Black, and because this activity was part of the school's Black History Month activities. If this kind of thing occurs in the program your child attends, you will need to educate the teacher, the program and the school.

Some schools tolerate a hostile environment against biracial and biethnic children. A White mother told me of problems her biracial kindergarten daughter was experiencing in the school she attended. The students said very hateful things to this young child about her White mother. When the mother reported this to the school, and asked for assistance in dealing with the problem, they refused to intercede.

If the center or school you are considering uses videos, make sure minorities are shown in a positive way, and that these videos show a variety of people.

Some early childhood and school programs only use minorities at the low end of their system - janitors, teacher assistants, cooks, etc. I would be reluctant to have my children attend such a program, because it models to the child that minorities cannot succeed, and it suggests the program does not promote minority workers, or hire them into important positions.

Observe the program in action. Talk to the teachers and the director. Talk to other parents. If the program will not let you come in and observe when you choose, don't consider it for your child. When observing the program, watch how children interact with each other; observe the discipline used by the teachers, and notice how they solve normal conflicts between children. Be particularly concerned if adults respond to minority children in a stereotypical manner, talk down to them, and generally treat them differently from the other children. The National Association for the Education of Young Children (NAEYC) accredits child care and early childhood programs. This accreditation is a good indicator of a quality program, but says little about its multiracial approach.

When you enroll your child, talk to the director about your child's identity, how you support that identity at home, and how you expect it to be supported at the center or school. Be wary of the common response, "We don't notice the differences in our children - we love them all and treat them alike." As pointed out earlier in this chapter, young children do notice differences. And we know teachers often respond to children differently, based on a teacher's own biases and the way they were raised. Do not assume teachers do not have their own biases, and act, even subconsciously, according to these biases. And don't assume a minority teacher will be better for your child than a White teacher. Because of the opposition to interracial and interethnic marriages by some minorities, minority teachers may dislike mixed- race children. Also many minorities have been raised to view biracial and biethnic child with the sole identity of their parent of color, and may respond to biracial children in their care in this way.

Many preschools, Head Start programs, family child care centers and public schools take racial and ethnic information on the children they enroll, to receive various forms of government assistance. Each interracial and interethnic family must decide how to deal with this issue. If the current system of collecting racial and ethnic data stands, you will have to address this issue on numerous occasions, for numerous programs, until your child leaves college. Presently none of these forms has a category for mixed-race children; a few allow parents to fill in "other", although these are being eliminated. As I pointed out earlier, the U.S. Census Committee has just approved a new policy allowing people to fill in more than one category on census forms. It is yet to be seen whether this approach will be used by children's programs when they collect ethnic and racial data.

Our family first encountered this issue when our second child was born, and the hospital asked what race we wanted on her birth certificate (with our first child we believe the hospital automatically filled in the Black category, without asking us). We told them biracial. The nurse said this was not a choice. Finally, after about 40 minutes of arguing, the nurse said, "Well, I'll put in race unknown." Since then we have filled in 'other' or left the space blank. Once our children became old enough, they filled in their own forms. Maia (our eldest) has declared that "I won't fill in 'other' because I am not an other; I am somebody."

Some interracial parents choose whatever category will give them the advantage they seek: if a school needs a White student, their child is White; if a minority student is required, then they fill in the category of the child's minority parent.

There are some facts about this issue that might help you make your decision:

.You do not have to fill out a category - or give the information to an official for them to fill out the form;

.The official cannot fill out a form in a way that you disagree with;

.Your child's program funding is not jeopardized by your refusal to fill out these forms;

.A program cannot refuse to serve your child if you choose not to fill in their forms.

If a program expresses frustration - or anger - at you for refusing to fill out these government forms, suggest they talk to their federal or school official. Let them know the current federal process does not meet your family's needs, and does not accurately reflect the racial and ethnic identity of your child.

Working with the school and child care

At the time you enroll your child in a school or early childhood program, let them know you are available as a resource to help them address the needs of your child and other mixed-race children in the program. You could also suggest resource materials for the classroom, speakers to visit the school, training for all the staff, and ongoing workshops. Once your child is enrolled, monitor the program through unannounced visits, talk to your child about his experiences at day care or school, provide suggestions of books, activities and resources, and activity ensure the program has a biracial and biethnic perspective.

Programs for high risk children

There is a growing trend in this country to try to identify high risk students early in their school or child care experience.

Further, there is an assumption that all young children - age 3 to 6- should essentially be at the same place in their development. Because many teachers and other school professionals (social workers, psychologists, and administrators) don't understand minority children, and may view mixed-race children as abnormal and messed up, they often identify these children as high risk. High risk means the child is more likely to have problems succeeding in school. You need to be aware of this tendency and make sure any school-based professionals evaluate your child's total abilities before making any decisions. For example, young boys (3-7) are generally academically and socially delayed compared to young girls. We also know young boys' activity level leads them to have more behavior problems in school than young girls. In the early grades far more boys than girls are placed in special education programs. There are many more boys diagnosed with ADD/ADHD (Attention Deficit Hyperactive Disorder) than girls. So be careful if you have a biracial or biethnic boy who the professionals tell you is delayed, high risk, hyperactive, and in need of special programs.

Information and training about the unique needs of minority families and individuals has only recently entered our professional schools. And none of these schools provide accurate training about mixed-race children. Because professionals receive no training about these children, or receive training that tells them these children will have problems, they often give parents inaccurate information. Some years ago I interviewed the Harvard psychiatrist Alvin Poussaint for a magazine article. I specifically asked Dr. Poussaint whether he still believed biracial children have problems, or if he changed his mind. Dr. Poussaint responded that his formal training taught him biracial children should have all sorts of problems, but his experience and research suggested otherwise. Another professional told a parent of an adopted biracial child that it is common knowledge biracial children have language delays.

Parents with biracial and biethnic children must be very

wary of misinformation from professionals. Often they don't know, or have the wrong information. Many professionals - and lots of the articles in professionals journals about mixed-race children - assume any problem a biracial or biethnic child has is the direct result of being mixed. Make sure you are involved in the evaluation process of your child. And make sure you know your rights as a parent.

Travel

Obviously my family values travel. Both Ruth and I have always liked to travel; we have continued this practice with our children. It's a tremendous way to expand the cultural horizons of children. Somehow it teaches them to be open to differences, to recognize people celebrate important events in different ways, and to enjoy different food, art, music, and dance. We have traveled to Pueblo Indian cliff dwellings, visited the Museum of Man in Winnipeg, toured Norman castles and Roman ruins in Wales, talked to Spanish American weavers in the villages high above Santa Fe, New Mexico, and visited the Hutterites and Amish in Pennsylvania. Our children spent two weeks in France several years ago; and my son recently spent 3 weeks playing soccer with some friends of mine in Brazil.

Working with professionals

Be careful of therapists who insist on making race the main issue in helping to solve your child's problems. Very rarely is race an issue that causes psychological problems at a young age (up to age 8). Make sure if you have a professional working with your child that she explores all other possible causes for the problem. Much of a young child's experience has nothing to do with their racial identity. This is also true for the biracial and biethnic child. These children experience all the challenges and problems all other

41

children experience. They should be explored first. It is therefore very important that parents, teachers and professionals do not make race an issue when it is not one. It is my experience biracial and biethnic children will bring up race if that is an issue for them.

If you or others introduce the child's mixed-race identity as the possible cause for all his problems, he will begin to believe that it is, in fact, a problem being biracial or biethnic. He might even use it as an excuse.

Support all forms of diversity

Interracial and interethnic families should find ways to celebrate all kinds of diversity, depending on their own interests and opportunities. I have already talked about attending a variety of festivals, and exposing my children to travel. They have also experienced a variety of folk dances from many different countries, and all except Maia attended a French school, where much of the curriculum was taught in French. Learning a second language - any second language - is a tremendous way to expand a child's cultural horizon. The diversity does not necessarily need to be directly connected with your family's heritage - any diversity is positive.

Conclusion

An interracial or interethnic home - whether biological, adoptive or blended - sets the cultural climate for your child. Like all homes, it is where the child develops her foundation for self acceptance, self-esteem, racial identity and pride, tolerance and enjoyment of diversity. Thus it is essential the home is not only a place where normal good child raising practices take place, but also where parents model acceptance of differences, ability to resolve conflicts, and - most critically - acceptance and support of both of the child's genetic and cultural backgrounds. The future happiness of biracial and biethnic children is set during the early years at home.

Chapter 3
Adopted Biracial Children

Parents who adopt biracial children have all the same challenges as interracial birth parents. Additionally they must address several other problems: overcoming the opposition by much of the adoption community to transracial adoption, responding to the general position of the adoption community that biracial and biethnic children must be raised as Black (or the identity of their parent of color), handling all the issues that come with any adoption, and raising a minority child in, usually, a White home. Many families that adopt biracial and biethnic children are White. Most of the advice in this chapter is for White families who adopt children of mixed heritage - both domestic and foreign. An adopted biracial or biethnic child from another country poses issues of national origin and culture, and possible forms of prejudice unique to the child's country of origin.

Adoption

There are many excellent books, magazine articles, and materials provided by adoption agencies, to help adoptive parents - both before they adopt, and once the child is part of their family. It is not my intent to cover all the information these documents discuss. I merely want to touch on some of the more common elements all adoptive parents must address, while concentrating on specific issues pertinent to adopted biracial and biethnic children.

Adopted children go through the same developmental stages and growing pains all children experience. Their first day of school or child care may be difficult, they must develop social skills and important childhood friendships, they need discipline and loving guidance, and they strive for a sense of belonging. An adopted child must also deal with the loss of his birth parents, wonder why he was given up for adoption, come to terms with memories of his foster care experiences, overcome abuse in some cases, and wonder whether his new family will reject him - especially when he gets himself into trouble. These concerns come and go. They are not handled once, then dismissed.

Each adopted child also has unique needs, depending on whether she was adopted as an infant or older child, whether she is from another country, and whether there are other children already in the home.

An adopted infant needs time to slowly bond with her new parents, have her parents adapt to her temperament, and respond to other unique needs. It is essential the adoptive parents don't expect the new arrival to change to their well organized and established lifestyle. They need to be prepared to change family schedules and long established family patterns. If this is their first child, they will experience all the changes biological families experience with their first child, but without the 9 months of pregnancy. Adoptive homes can, of course, be two parent homes or single parent (male or female) homes.

An infant needs lots of sleep, gentle handling, and a schedule that matches her needs with those of her parents.

An older adopted child has to cope with a total change of the environment he is used to. Family, neighborhood, extended family and school are all new. It's important these environments support the adopted child - especially if he is from a different country, or racial background. A full time parent at home (father or mother) helps provide some stability, at least for the first weeks of the adoption. Government leave policies now enable a new adoptive parent to stay at home, if he or she so chooses. Some families delay enrollment of their older adopted children into the school until they have become comfortable with the family and community.

If the adoptive family has children, they should be involved in the adoption process, and fully prepared for the new arrival - just as one prepares birth children for a new sibling. Never should the existing children (biological or adopted) feel the new child is an imposition or competition. If the child is from another country they should be encouraged to do research on that country - music, dance, language, history, culture, geography and food. They can view the new child as an opportunity to learn more about the richness and excitement of the world.

In our family we developed a ritual for the birth of each new child. The new baby would give a gift to her siblings. In this way not all the attention and gift giving were going to the baby, setting up jealousy with the other children. We also included our children in preparing for their new sibling - everything from visiting the hospital before the birth, to preparing her room at home. This idea could be used when adopting a child into a family that already has children.

Between the ages of 3 to 5 years old, many adopted children begin to become interested in their backgrounds. The healthiest approach to an adopted child's curiosity is to answer questions openly and simply. As with the issue of biracial and biethnic identity, children this age can, to some extent, understand the concept of adoption. If this information is handled positively by the family, the child is able to explore and resolve the issues that concern adopted children, especially the belief that somehow they caused their birth parents to give them up for adoption: that it was their fault.

Many adoptive families celebrate the day their child entered their home, or the day the adoption process was made final, as a second birthday. This legitimizes the adoption and also makes the adopted child feel special.

All adopted children naturally want to know about their parents. "What was my other mother like?" "What about my other father - do I look like him?" Tell them what you know - as simply and straightforwardly as possible. Also try to make it as positive as possible. If the child is the result of a non-loving relationship, and/or given up because the parent(s) couldn't handle raising a biracial or biethnic child, it is often difficult to say much that is positive. Unfortunately some adopted biracial and biethnic children are given up for adoption as a result of a negative experience: taken away from their parents by social services, or because of racism. Sometime the mother will give up the child because she does not have the family support to raise a mixed-race child in a racist society.

Advice from other adoptive parents, support groups, and professionals in the field will help with these difficult situations. Private adoption agencies and public agencies (social services) provide training and support groups for adoptive parents - especially those engaged in transracial adoption. Almost all the interracial support groups throughout the country include families who have transracially adopted children - both domestic and foreign.

When adopted children reach their teens many become interested in searching for their birth parents. This is a natural process that shouldn't be viewed as a rejection of the adoptive family. Adoptive parents who support their children's natural curiosity about their roots often find it a positive experience for them and their children. However, it is important this is done in a healthy way. Biracial and biethnic children's cultural roots include a vast amount of cultural background, depending on the heritage of both biological parents.

Adoptive families have experienced the need to educate professionals and the public about their unique status. They still find there is a need for more education of the public about adoption. Schools, universities, the media, childcare programs, social workers, and school counselors all need constant information to destroy myths and help them meet the needs of adopted children and adoptive families.

Opposition to transracial adoption

There is considerable opposition in this country to transracial adoption - the adoption of minority children into White homes. Historically the adoption community assumed that matching a child's physical characteristics (not just racial) to those of the adoptive parents would go a long way in assuring the success of the adoption. Later minority groups became concerned about minority children being raised without any sense of their cultural history. As a result, Native American Nations pushed for legislation to control adoption of children from their tribes. Then, in 1972 the National Association of Black Social Workers (NABSW) adopted a statement declaring vehement opposition to the practice of placing Black children in White homes. They reaffirmed this official position in 1977 and 1985. The association charged transracial adoption would lead to the genocide of the Black race. Shortly after this position was taken, the authoritative Child Welfare League of America revised its standards to support same race adoptions (although later it qualified this position). Now almost all public adoption agencies, and many private ones, along with adoption magazines and books, officially or unofficially oppose transracial adoption.

Technically a biracial child adopted by a White family is no more a transracial adoption than a biracial child adopted by a Black family. But, since much of society still views biracial children as Black, and almost all of the adoption community view biracial children as Black, adoption of a biracial child by a White home is usually viewed as a transracial adoption.

Many states and the federal government have addressed the issue of transracial adoption - in various ways - to try to provide official guidelines for this emotional issue. Minnesota's Heritage Preservation Act (passed in 1983; amended in 1993) requires social service agencies in that state to search for relatives or families of the same race/ethnic background of the child, before considering transacial adoption. A Texas law, passed in 1993, states that the race of a child cannot be given any more weight than any other factor, when considering placement.

The federal law, The Multiethnic Placement Act (sponsored by Howard Metzenbaum), states that while same race placements are preferable, race cannot be the sole consideration in making foster care and adoption placements. If it is agencies could lose federal funding.

The impact of these laws on transacial adoption depends largely on the politics of the interpreter and the hidden agendas of those involved. Randall Kennedy, a Black Professor of Law at Harvard University, believes the federal legislation will actually enable social workers who oppose transacial adoption to keep minority children in institutions and foster care longer than necessary; the 1997 Annual Conference of the Child Welfare League includes a session that indicates these laws will prevent, "successful placement" of Black children.

Race is still used by many agencies and adoption organizations as a major factor in placing minority children, including biracial and biethnic children. I have a friend who is a White foster mother who provides emergency foster care for Denver Social Services. Social workers continually criticize and harass her for caring for biracial and Black infants. And when the children are ready for adoption, she is told by these social workers that they look for adoptive parents with the same skin color (amount of pigment) as that of the child. This is in a state - Colorado - that has a statute outlawing delays in adoption because of race.

Opposition to transacial adoption has become part of many groups' political agendas. A White family wishing to adopt a biracial or biethnic child (domestic or foreign) must be aware of this situation. It will make the process more difficult, and will place undue scrutiny on the family as the child grows older. Their continual relationship with adoption professionals - for support, advice, and financial assistance - will always be influenced by this particular bias, as will their relationship with other professionals. White families adopting transracially must be secure in their beliefs about adoption, sophisticated in working with social service professionals, able to seek advice from outside the traditional adoption community, and assertive in their approach to raising these children. They must also be committed to expose their adopted children to the child's culture and heritage.

The research is very clear about the success of transracial adoption. Minority children raised in White homes are as successful as same race, minority, adopted children and birth children, and, if these children are exposed to aspects of their cultural and national heritage in a constant, positive, meaningful way, they develop a strong pride in their cultural and racial heritage. White parents can teach Black children a healthy sense of identity and nondiscriminatory attitudes. Research also suggests transracially adopted children grow up with more acceptance and tolerance for people of different racial and ethnic backgrounds.

Adoption community views biracial children as Black

Prospective White parents who wish to adopt biracial or biethnic children must aggressively address the question of the identity of their child. In chapter one I discuss the issues around the identity of biracial and biethnic children. In chapter two I presented ideas for how families can support this identity. These ideas apply also to adopted biracial and biethnic children. Additionally, the adoptive parent should read books on the subject, join groups that share your position (or start your own) and subscribe to interracial newsletters and magazines. Find other adoptive families with biracial and biethnic children. Talk to birth families with mixed-race children. And be skeptical of the advice of psychologists and social workers.

Make no mistake, if you raise your adopted child as biracial or biethnic, you will be accused by some in the adoption community of many things. The *Adoptive Child Newsletter* accuses White parents who raise their adopted children as biracial of trying to claim their child, of having ulterior motives (all sorts, including trying to reduce tension between the races), of trying to distance themselves from the child's Black heritage, of being unrealistic, and of putting an undue burden on an already over burdened child (adopted and a minority). These parents are accused of denying their child a group to belong to, setting the child up for psychological failure, and teaching the child there is something wrong with being Black (or the ethnic group of their parent of color).

Supporting the identity of an adopted biracial or biethnic child

Parents of an adopted biracial child have a three-fold task: to help the child feel good about being adopted, to raise a minority child in, usually, a White home, and to develop a healthy biracial or biethnic identity in their child. These challenges are in addition to the challenges all parents face in raising healthy children in America today.

In addition to issues around this topic already discussed in the book, the White adoptive family must understand that by adopting one or more minority children they have become a minority family. Further - given the misunderstanding about adoption by much of society - the home is a double minority home. This means the family will need to undergo changes to meet the needs of their minority children. It also means the family must actively support their role as an open, accepting island in an often racist sea of society. You must be able to discuss racism, prejudice, fear of the unknown, adoption, nationalism, rejection, loyalty, and cultural barriers, in your home. The White home that has adopted biracial or biethnic children needs to make a special effort to provide their children with minority contacts and modeling. This can be done through family friends, joining groups, living in an integrated neighborhood, and attending integrated early childhood programs and schools. But be careful! Almost all White families who adopt transracially are middle class. Don't assume you should expose your adopted biracial children to inner-city activities and institutions. Be involved with minorities in your community, your professional organizations, your neighborhood soccer teams and schools.

What is important to recognize is that your children have identity issues that are different from White children and single-race minority children. And - since neither of you are a minority - you do not have the knowledge needed to help your child in this area. But you can learn it!

Families with minority children must find ways to expose their children to children like them, from an early age. You might have to move, you might have to drive further to a school or child care center, you might have to recruit other families of color to your school, neighborhood, church, or social group. Often interracial support groups serve this important function.

As discussed in other sections of this book, calendars, posters, magazines, art work, music, dance, children's books, children's magazines, and picture books in your home must reflect your minority child's membership in your family, and that his minority status (history, physical characteristics, and culture) is interwoven into the cultural fabric of your home. Mirrors, opportunities to use art materials (especially mixing of paints), dress-up clothes and various hair brushes, ribbons, barrettes, etc., will help your child explore her physical features. Different foods, and even learning your child's original language, can be important.

But don't ignore your own heritage. It's important that your biracial or biethnic child learns about your heritage, learns your customs and celebrations, and knows you are proud of your own background. And if your child has some White heritage, she needs to learn about that side of her identity, too. And she needs to learn that you and she have that heritage in common.

While your mixed-race child will experience biases and racism in the neighborhood, school and peer groups (from both

Whites, minorities, and institutions in general), most experiences she has will have little to do with race. When she comes to you with problems, don't automatically assume they are caused by her racial identity or her being adopted.

Your child is part of your family

While it is obvious an adopted child of mixed heritage is in many ways different from her parents and siblings, especially in a White family, and that people outside of the family will concentrate on these differences, make every effort to help her feel part of your family. She does have many things in common with you: both of you belong to the same family, both of you have needs and wishes, both of you experience joys and sorrows, and both of you have some White heritage and culture.

Fourteen Ways for Adoptive Families to Face the Challenges in Everyday Lives (By Tara Tieso-Battis, used by permission. First published in *New People*, 1992).

. Always believe your child when he/she tells you they have been the victim of bias (warped or prejudiced thinking about an object, issue or group of people).

. Acknowledge that many people in your own community, and indeed the world, do sometimes behave in a biased manner toward those they perceive as different. Validate.

. Educate your child about this fact early in their lives, so they will be less likely to take biased behavior personally.

. Help your child understand their words, actions or reactions have nothing to do with the biased behaviors of others, and they bear no responsibility for the ignorance of others.

. Make an effort to discover the things you don't know first-hand about racism. What you don't know can hurt your kids.

. Know that despite all you may do to educate and help a child understand racism, bias will hurt them deeply, and leave an impression.

. Remember, as a parent in a "different" family, you too will likely become a victim of bias.

. Recognize your own "old tapes" and learn to see your own subtle bias. ("Too many chiefs, and not enough Indians," Polish jokes, telling a spouse they have Alzheimers in response to a forgetful act.) Try to provide a positive example of non-biased behaviors.

. Never underestimate the power of your response to biased acts when you are in the presence of your children. Kids learn most from your example (both positive and negative). Walk your talk.

. Give your child a positive feeling about their community of color, the country of their birth, those in the community living with similar special needs, and others who have become a family through adoption. These feelings are an important part of your child's core of self-worth.

. Increase your circle of friends to include a wide diversity of people. You can walk up to someone and say, "Will you be my friend?"

. Remember your responsibility to help your child grow into an adult with a positive self-identity extends to your community, and the greater world. Think globally - act locally!

. Tell your kids often that you are proud to be their parent, that they have made a profound difference in your life - and they will know they can make a difference in the world.

. Self-esteem begins in the arms of those who love us - kiss, hug and say, "I love you!" over and over again.

Adopted foreign biracial and biethnic children

Adopted biracial and biethnic children from other countries pose additional challenges. The main need is to include their nation of origin as part of their identity. Parents must become familiar with the nation: customs, history, language, art, music, food, and religion. They also need to know the status of mixed race children in that country. Some foreign countries - such as Korea and Vietnam - totally disown mixed-race children, while others - like Brazil and Mexico- have a rich history of considering mixed-race people part of their overall population. All countries have their own unique approachs (and prejudices) to race, ethnicity, mixed-race people, and nationalism. Like the U.S., all other countries have subgroups within them that are culturally different from the majority. Find out all you can about the subgroup your child is from, if he is not from the majority culture. Most of these countries are far more concerned with national identity than racial labels. Compared to other countries, the United States is particularly ridged regarding racial labels, mixed-race identity, and racial politics.

Sometimes the exact heritage of a foreign, mixed-race child is not known. This makes supporting your child's total genetic heritage difficult.

Include the knowledge you have of your child's national (and maybe tribal) heritage in the culture of your home: food, music, art, geography, books, National Geographic articles, PBS programs, folk dances, reports at school, national and folk heroes, and information about the past and present role of the U.S. in his country. While your child is now a U. S. citizen, his national origin is a critical part of his heritage, and will always be a part of him. And if your child's heritage includes minority status within the country - say a Native tribe - find out specific cultural and historical information about that tribe.

A foreign adopted, biracial or biethnic child is different from a child of similar racial and ethnic heritages born in this country. This is even truer if you raise your biracial child as Black. A Black child from Kenya has little in common with a Black child from Washington, D.C. A biracial, Black/White child from Brazil has little in common with an American Black/White biracial child. Your foreign biracial child must learn to relate to these American-born biracial children and American minority children, learn about American prejudices, color sensitivity, and national myopia, and learn to protect himself. But don't force your child to feel he is the same as these children. He is not.

Many common issues face adoptive parents of domestic and foreign biracial children. I have already discussed the critical need for these children to be given accurate information about their total heritage, and to have their minority status celebrated and supported.

All parents of adopted children must respond to insensitive questions from curious strangers. Parents of adopted children who don't look like their parents have added questions, comments and looks from strangers to cope with. "What is his race?" "He must look like his father, (mother)." Or, "So, you adopted a Black baby, how nice", are typical of these comments.

You have no obligation to give out information about your adopted children. This is personal information. However, you need to make sure your child - especially as she grows older - doesn't think you are not giving out information about her (adopted, race, nation of origin) because you are ashamed of her background or origin.

Your response will probably depend on the motivation of the questions asked. If it is mean, then tell them it is none of their business. If it is genuine, then respond in kind.

However, it is critical for your adopted child that interactions with others do not focus on differences between him and his family. He needs to know he is a baby like all other babies - smiles, cries, gets hungry, etc. Try to steer conversations by others about your child into discussions that reinforce he is your child, you are his parent, and that the interactions between the two of you are like that of other parents and their infants (or older children).

Conclusion

The politics of race in this country adds additional pressure to White families adopting minority children. This is made even more complicated if the child is biracial, biethnic, and/or from another country. Adoptive parents need to recognize these challenges, seek out accurate information, and join support groups to empower them to be good parents. But focusing on these real dilemmas should not prevent adoptive parents from raising their children with all the love, support, joy, advice, care, nurturing, and passion that all children need. The secret to raising adopted biracial and biethnic children is to provide a healthy, open, secure home where the child's racial and national heritage is an integral part of the values and environment.

Chapter 4
Supporting Interracial Families in Early Childhood Programs and Schools

Interracial and interethnic families need sensitive, continuous support from all professionals, including teachers and administrators. These families struggle with the issues and challenges all American family face - finances, jobs, relatives, domestic disagreements, schools and child care - and additional problems specific to their family's uniqueness. These problems may include one or more of the following: harassment from the public; harassment of their children in school, child care and the community; lack of support from relatives; lack of a sense of community, and professionals who are either insensitive to their specific problems, or openly biased against them.

    The early childhood program and school play a critical role in the healthy development of biracial and biethnic children. A child's sense of identity - including recognition of physical characteristics - begins to be formed during the early childhood years. It continues through adolescence, where racial identity is one of several critical challenges the child must address. So it is essential the child care program, preschool and school positively support the biracial and biethnic child and her family. These programs are the primary place where children receive social feedback about who they are: their physical appearance, language, home, physical and intellectual abilities, and their own self-image. Often a child learns racial stereotypes from experiences in these programs; or has his own fears and narrow perceptions of others confirmed.

    A positive attitude toward mixed-race children and their families must exist in the entire early childhood program and school. This attitude must be established by the director or principal and school counselors, who should create a climate that celebrates diversity of all children and their families. Training, posters, staff attitudes and communication, art work, and staffing, will need to reflect this richness and diversity. Interracial and interethnic families must feel they belong in the program; they must feel the program supports their choice of a partner, the way they choose to raise their children, and the daily struggles they experience to provide what is best for their children. If these families only see photos and posters in the school and child care program of single race families, they will learn the program does not recognize and validate them. Biracial and biethnic children will begin to believe there is something wrong with themselves and their families.

Teacher's support of children of mixed heritage

A teacher's support of any individual difference in her classroom starts with her own understanding and comfort level with differences. Does she respect the individual rights of children with a disability, without pitying them? Does she sincerely believe a mixed-race child in her classroom can be as successful as any other child? Is she sympathetic to the needs of the abused child? How well does she relate to the adopted child? Does she unconsciously believe in the stereotypes about minorities (for example, expecting all Asian children to be good at math, expecting a Black boy to be athletic)?

Teachers must explore their feelings about biracial and biethnic children; they must examine their reaction to these children and their parents. Do they feel interracial relationships are somehow unnatural and unhealthy? Are they uneasy around these families? Do they insist the biracial child is Black, even when the parent chooses to raise him as biracial? And, most importantly, does she automatically conclude any problems this child has is due to his mixed-race status?

Training

To help teachers explore their attitudes, be supportive of these children and their families, and recognize how biracial and biethnic children can positively impact their classrooms, the child care program and school should provide training to all teachers and counselors. Experts should assist teachers in addressing issues of racism, myths about this population, and personal prejudices. Accurate information must be provided, and parent's wishes respected.

While minority teachers usually have a different perception than White teachers regarding interracial relationships and mixed-race children, they still come to this issue with a history of preconceptions. Also, White teachers often seek out advice from single race minority professionals about biracial and biethnic children and their families. Because of the current trends of supporting ethnic and racial pride, the stress of developing a healthy ethnic and racial identity in all of our children, and a belief in the importance of reference group orientation, some minority teachers and minority professionals are opposed to interracial and interethnic relationships and biracial and biethnic children. They believe these children must be raised as a member of their minority parent's group. In fact, my family has received more opposition to our advocacy of raising children with a healthy biracial identity from minority professionals than from White professionals.

The trainer of these sessions needs to understand factors that impact minorities in our society: power, accessibility, prejudice, harassment and history. She must understand how these pressures are perpetuated within our educational institutions. The trainer must also have a clear understanding that interracial and interethnic families and their children must deal with prejudice, harassment and disownership from the majority and minority communities. Finally, the trainer must believe these parents have the right and responsibility to raise their children as they choose;

and that schools and child care programs must support this choice and provide expert assistance.

The racial and cultural background of the trainer is not as important as her knowledge of the issues, support of teachers exploring their own biases, and sympathy for the rights and struggles of interracial and interethnic families.

I recently attended a national training presented by the consultant for a state department of education. This trainer works directly with teachers throughout the state, teaching them how to adapt the curriculum, classrooms, and activities to support minority children's healthy identity development and academic success. Her presentation provided expert advice. Then she addressed the needs of Black/White biracial children. She insisted these children are Black, must be raised as Black, and that teachers and parents who believe otherwise need to be educated about race and identity in America.

Content of staff training will differ, depending on the institution and age of students. Generally it should include: exploring individual and institutional prejudice; a history of multiracial people in this country and the world; a discussion of the biological and socio-political concept of race (in this and other countries); identity development of all children, minority children, and biethnic and biracial children; the development and politics of the Census Bureau and O.M.B. categories; pressure faced by interracial families; community and educational resources, and specific suggestion of how teachers and schools can support interracial and interethnic families. This latter point can be further explored by inviting local resource people to the training, and by using parents as trainers and providers of reference materials.

A section of the training should also be devoted to why current multicultural educational models do not include biracial and biethnic children, and how these models need to be changed to include this ever increasing population.

Initial parent-teacher conference

At the initial parent-teacher conference, discuss with parents of biracial and biethnic children the issue of identity. How is the child's identity viewed in the home? How is that identity cultivated and supported? How do parents want it to be supported in the classroom and school? Also determine how parents respond to negative comments directed at their children - from other children and adults. What do they tell their children to say? How do they affirm their child's positive differences?

While you need to honor and respect the parent's wishes in the approach they use to identify their child, also provide them with information about supporting their child's full racial and cultural identity. Let them know that it's OK to raise their child as biracial or biethnic; and that, even if they wish to raise their child with the single identity of their minority parent, it is healthy for the child to understand, appreciate, and have pride in both sides of his heritage. Provide the parents with books and articles about mixed-race identity, the current multiracial movement, and local support groups.

Don't jump to conclusions

Interracial and interethnic families face all the issues other families face. And - most of the time - the issues that preoccupy them have nothing to do with being a mixed- race family. It is critically important teachers and other professionals working with these families don't automatically assume problems or concerns they might have are caused by their racial, ethnic or adoptive status. One of the things interracial and interethnic families are super-sensitive about is professionals who immediately assume a mixed-race child is having behavioral or academic problems because she is biracial or biethnic. Or that an interracial couple is having marital problems because of their racial differences. Or a biracial child has low self-esteem because she is, "Not in touch with her Blackness."

If a biracial or biethnic child has a problem, find out what the parents consider to be causing it. Ask as many questions as you need to. Explore all other options, including possible testing, if needed, before considering that the problem may be because the family is racially mixed. Don't play amateur psychologist; and don't allow professional psychologists to jump to biased conclusions. Remember few psychologists have training and experience working with interracial families and transracial adoptive families.

Curriculum materials

One of the central problems in meeting the needs of interracial and interethnic families in our early childhood programs and schools is an almost total lack of curriculum materials. There are no posters of multiracial heroes; no biographies of famous multiracial and multiethnic Americans; no mixed-race doll families; almost no puzzles or posters of these families; few story books that address this issues; and few educational books and articles on multicultural education that include the needs of interracial and interethnic families and their children.

Teachers need to be very persistent in demanding that early childhood and school supply companies start meeting the needs of these families. Ask your vendors for materials. Ask your book store. Ask the companies that produce curriculum and classroom materials. Most of these companies believe there is no need to provide these materials (thus they cannot make any money providing them). They believe this because O.M.B. and census figures don't count biracial and biethnic children, because teachers and administrators don't demand them, and because traditional multicultural curricular lump biracial and biethnic children into the racial or ethnic group of the child's parent of color.

Also, whenever teachers attend workshops or conferences

on multicultural education and diversity in the classroom, they should request that sessions on the unique needs of interracial and interethnic families and their children be provided. This should also be demanded of professionals who provide multicultural training to local child care programs and schools. We can no longer ignore this population - especially within the context of multicultural education, diversity in the classroom, and equal educational access to all children in our programs.

Group antagonism

While many interracial and interethnic families receive full support from their extended families and communities, others are fairly isolated. They may have lost relative support - on one or both sides of the family - and they may not have full support of their communities - neighbors, church, scouts, after school programs, and sports teams. Some mixed-race families, especially when they start out, feel isolated and alone. They receive harassment - directly and indirectly - from both the minority and White communities. They almost always are stared at, sometimes rudely. As I have also pointed out, these families may also experience difficulties with professionals in their lives - psychologists, social workers, teachers, group facilitators, trainers and others. Because of this isolation and harassment, interracial and interethnic parents are often super-sensitive. They may over-react - especially to situations they believe to be biased, prejudicial or unfair.

Teachers and school administrators can offset this situation by providing sensitive support to these families. Listen to their issues. Respond sincerely. Try to rectify real problems. Refer parents to support groups if there are any in your area. Many foster and adoptive agencies provide educational support groups that address issues important to interracial and interethnic families (self-esteem, identity development, resisting harassment, minority issues). If there are several mixed-race families in your program or school, help them set up their own support group (provide a place to meet, resources, resource people, and publications).

Never blame parents for problems they have, or their children have, with comments or implications that they brought on these problems by crossing the racial and ethnic taboo to marry and have children, adopted transracially, or that they are selfish to have biracial or biethnic children in a racist society. These families need - and deserve - support, resources, responsive environments, and assistance from teachers, administrators and support professionals

Racial categories

I have discussed the lack of a biracial, biethnic, multiethnic or multiracial category on census and government forms. Many interracial and interethnic parents first experience this official denial of their child's identity when they enroll them in an early childhood program or school. I have heard many horror stories about this dilemma from across the country.

Each program must determine the best way to handle racial categories on forms. Whatever you decide, it must be done with sensitivity and understanding. Some programs allow parents to fill in the choice they select, whatever that is. Talk to your funding officer if you have a problem, and explore all possible options. Also openly discuss with the parents what approach they wish to take. However, be aware that you cannot force a parent to select a category for their child they do not choose; and you cannot refuse entrance to your program of a child whose parent will not fill out the forms.

Help interracial families explore their heritage

Child care programs and schools can be a great impetus for interracial families to embrace their total heritage, and for the program or school to celebrate their commitment to diversity. Encourage all parents to visit ethnic stores, attend cultural festivals, and explore their family's rich heritage, be it Hispanic, Black, Irish, Lithuanian, or multiracial or multiethnic. Invite interracial and interethnic parents - along with other parents who bring a diverse perspective to your program - to help you construct a truly anti-bias, multicultural curriculum. And invite mixed-race, mixed-nationality, and mixed-religion couples to assist in training of staff about the needs of mixed-race children.

Help these families find books, dolls, stories and other resources. Help them utilize the community. If they need professional help for their child, help them find professionals who are sensitive to their needs, supportive of their right to develop a healthy family, and understanding of the unique identity needs of biracial and biethnic children. Central to this effort is the program's view of race. If the program believes in the concept that the world's population can be broken into neat, exclusive racial and ethnic categories - Black, Hispanic (Latino), Native American, White and Asian - then the mixed-race child (biological and adopted) will never feel fully accepted in the school.

Specific school and classroom suggestions

There are specific things an early childhood program and school can do to support the biracial and biethnic child. Of most importance is that the entire family feels welcome in the program. Then there are specific classroom activities that can be included in the curriculum.

Classroom materials. Through stories, role playing, videos, photos, picture books, and doll sets, the teacher can show his students how people in this country have effectively mixed religions, national heritages and ethnic, racial, political and linguistic differences through marriage. Use a child with English/Polish parents to show how mixtures in marriage are popular and acceptable.

Family tree. Develop a family tree for each child in your classroom - going back as far as you can with each side of the child's heritage. Note the differences and origins of each child: nation, language, culture, and racial and tribal groups. Use photos and artifacts, and encourage parents, grandparents and other relatives to come to the classroom and talk with the children. The best way to initiate this activity is to send home questionnaires to parents and get specific information and materials. Obviously care must be taken with adopted and foster and children, and children from single parent homes. Work closely with the child's legal parents and social service agencies to provide as much information as possible. Make sure the activity is not designed in such a way that adopted children or other children who don't know both their parents, all their grandparents, etc., do not feel inferior. Older children can do oral and written reports, interviews, genealogical research, and integrated historic projects.

Encourage discussion. Encourage and support discussions about individual differences. Children are very curious; they also are uncertain and sometimes scared of the unknown. Openly respond to any questions about race, skin color, hair texture, eye shape, language difference and cultural traditions. Use the natural interest in these differences to talk about children getting their physical characteristic from their biological parents, learning family and cultural traditions from both sides of their background, and eventually developing their own sense of belonging and direction. And discuss how all children are the same: they receive love, support, modeling, and nurturing from all parents - biological, foster and adoptive. This activity will naturally lead into a project on different families. Develop a bulletin board, collage, individual journal or research project showing every variety of family - foster, adoptive, two parent, single female headed family, single male headed family, interracial, interethnic, extended, minority, and interfaith family. Also invite as many of these families to visit your classroom as possible.

Avoid a single race approach. Avoid curriculum materials, books, discussions and activities that divide the country and the world into neat, distinctive racial and ethnic categories. This is very easy to do because children are generalists who like to put the real world into neat categories, because teachers want to expose children to the variety of ethnic and racial groups that make up this country, and because the approach to diversity in this country focuses on belonging to distinct racial and ethnic groups. We need to help children view all people by their individual strengths and weaknesses. In supporting the richness and diversity of individual differences in our classrooms and the world, we cannot make the mistake of placing all people into neat, exclusive groups, based on physical characteristics or socio-political agendas.

Provide activities that build positive self-image. Provide lots of activities for mixing colors: paint, food colors, colored plastic, tissue paper, etc. Then have students use this new found skill to match paint mixtures with colors in their environment, including their own skin and hair color. They will discover that most colors in the environment are mixed, not pure, and that the natural world is made up of a rich variety of hues, shades, and subtle color combinations.

Older children can study the development of hybrids in plants and animals, and how scientists have combined genetic materials to create new, different, more hardy, and more environmentally resistant plants, crops and animals.

Provide many activities where children learn about their own physical characteristics, and learn to feel positive about those characteristics: drawing and painting pictures, making collages, viewing in the mirror, making life-size cutouts from butcher paper, and then filling in the correct flesh tone colors, and researching famous people of mixed cultural and genetic heritage. Make a big poster or bulletin board showing all the people in your program (children, teachers, cooks, bus drivers, principals), with a caption that conveys, "The Beauty of All People." Older children can make posters of photos and drawings of people in the neighborhood, bring in historic information from their families, and conduct reports of significant events in their families' history.

Avoid the tourist approach. Avoid only studying Hispanics at Cinco de Mayo time; only studying Indian Nations at Thanksgiving; studying Blacks only during Black History Month, and conveying that all Native Americans are all the same. The tourist approach to multicultural education presents racial and ethnic groups and international diversity through traditional dress, race-specific celebrations and dances, and culturally specific foods. At best it teaches children that minorities just celebrate and wear ceremonial costumes; at worst it perpetuates stereotypes, especially the stereotypes that people who belong to distinct ethnic and racial groups are all the same. An added problem with this approach for biracial and biethnic children is that they don't have a traditional reference group, so they are either ignored, or forced to identify only with the minority side of their parentage. Food, dress and celebrations are part of every person's background. These should be integrated into the overall curriculum.

Stress how we are all the same. Conduct classroom activities that address the commonality of all children in your program. Do a collage of hands, a poster of heads; have all children trace (or use as prints) their feet on butcher paper; construct a chart of emotions all children experience; initiate an activity exploring things we all have in common: parents, families, hopes, wishes, dreams, appetites, fears, and abilities.

Provide activities that illustrate non-racial/ethnic differences between children in your classroom: height, weight, likes, dislikes, jumping abilities, size of feet, size of hands, parents' occupations, ball catching and kicking abilities. Also include individual talents: playing an instrument, gymnastics, and singing, for example.

Invite a diversity of people to your classroom, especially those who challenge stereotypes. My wife and I became very upset when the Denver Public school our children were attending invited a Black football player to the school as a role model to discuss the value of staying in school. This player was widely known (also by the students) to have been convicted of wife abuse. He was not a good role model for our two daughters at that school. Invite Black professionals, White male ballet dancers, women CEOs, Hispanic business leaders, Native American mathematicians, and multiracial and multiethnic adults who have explored their rich heritage and history.

Be careful with language. Minorities, women and people with disabilities have educated us regarding the negative power of language. However, we have not addressed the problems that exist around the language used to describe interracial, interethnic and adoptive families, and their children. Be careful when taking about these families. Words like, "mixed up", "mulatto", "cultural margins", "marginal", "real parents", "confused", "identity dilemma", and "out-marriage", all convey negative assumptions about interracial, interethnic, and adoptive families. Even phases like racial and ethnic pride, racial and ethnic identity, and reference group orientation, can have a negative impact in child care programs, schools, or teacher training sessions, if it is assumed these words only apply to a single race or ethnicity (which they usually do).

Don't tolerate negative behavior toward biracial or biethnic children. Do not allow any child to say something negative to a biracial or biethnic child based on the child's physical characteristics or mixed heritage (obviously you should not allow this kind of behavior toward any child in your program or school). Find out the real reason for the comment or behavior, ("Well, he stole my truck," "She never plays fair," etc.). If a child continues to make negative comments, respond as you would to any unacceptable classroom or playground behavior (including talking to the child's parents.)

Provide activities that show variability within categories. Develop a chart of all the reds that children can find in the classroom (construction paper, magazine photos, cloth, paints, paint samples, food coloring, felt pens, children's clothing). A collage of different dogs, an art activity showing a variety of houses, and a fashion project showing different ethnic clothing are all examples of using categories to show diversity. Older children can conduct activities around the variability within scientific groupings of birds, animals, flowers and tress. For example, chart and illustrate the variety of maple trees.

Use the teachable moment. Children are very observant, and ask questions about things that confuse and interest them. Use these natural moments to help children appreciate diversity that they are not used to. If you see children from different ethnic and racial groups playing mother and father in the dramatic play area, and a child objects, use this incident as an opportunity to talk about how people from a variety of backgrounds marry and raise children. Or maybe you will observe a child who doesn't speak English trying to talk to another child. Again, you can discuss how there are many different languages in the world, including sign language, and how this makes it such a fascinating and rich place. Suggest to the child that she might be interested in learning a new language.

Contemporary conflicts around the world caused by racial and ethnic groupings, histories and loyalties, can be explored by older students to evaluate the problems associated with a stress on single ethnicity, race, language and tribal affiliation.

Help biracial and biethnic children stand up for themselves. I have already discussed the importance of a label or word for biracial and biethnic children to use to define and denfend themselves. Biracial and biethnic children need to know from the teacher that it's OK to be different; that differences make the world a richer place, and that, in most ways, they are no different from the other children. Teachers must also actively help children defend themselves (with verbal comments, etc.), and teachers must directly intervene, if necessary.

Interracial and interethnic families are an asset to your program

These families, along with other minority families, children with disabilities, and children who come from other countries, help a program and classroom to explore diversity. This is very positive, and will prepare all the children in the program and school to be successful and happy in the ever more diverse world.

Role models

One of the ultimate challenges in raising healthy biracial and biethnic children is that, because we do not recognize multiracial people in this country, our children do not see any role models. Even though people like Frederick Douglass, James Audubon and Maria Tallchief are multiracial and multiethnic, they are presented to our children as people with a single racial heritage. Our children have no sense of the history of biracial and biethnic people. See if there are role models in your school or program (multiracial and multiethnic adults, older children, parents); seek out people in your community who are proud of their multiracial heritage; research books on multiracial and multiethnic people. Maybe the older children can put together a book about some of these people.

Conclusion

Interracial and interethnic families must deal with all the stress and pressure other families face. Additionally they often face issues because they have challenged society's taboos to marry and have children across racial and ethnic lines. These stresses often include isolation, harassment, and lack of support - from relatives, in the community, and at school. Thus interracial and interethnic families need child care programs and schools that are sensitive, supportive, and treat them as sincere parents committed to raising healthy children in an unhealthy society. A child's positive identity at this age is directly tied to how he feels about his physical characteristics, how he feels about his family and friends, and what he can do (art, music, reading, climbing, and school subjects). So the most important thing a program or school and its staff can do is to make sure children of mixed heritage and their families feel totally accepted.

Chapter 5
Multiracial/Multiethnic Children Whose Parents Are Not Black/White

Introduction

Most interracial and interethnic families in this country are comprised of parents who are not Black and White. There are families of every conceivable combination: Native American, Black; Latino, White; Asian, White; Asian, Black; Hispanic, Native American; Black, Hispanic; and Native American, White. And we have interracial and interethnic families of partners who fall within the broad racial categories: Japanese, Korean; Mexican, Paraguayan; Mexican, Puerto Rican; African, Caribbean; Scottish, Italian, and, of course, inter-tribal marriages. And there are racial and ethnic groups within other nations, who marry each other: in Brazil there are Portuguese, Black, Indian, Asian, and multiracial people. We also have a rich history in this country of parents from different religious backgrounds raising children; the most obvious being Christian/Jewish homes. But when interracial families and biracial children are discussed, Black/White families and their children are usually the first to come to mind, because they challenge the most deep seated taboos in our country, and seem to be the most obvious example of "crossing the racial divide." And biracial, Black/White children do have unique and challenging needs. But - to some extent - any child whose parents come from different racial, ethnic, geographic, national, linguistic, tribal and religious groups are faced with many of the same issues as Black/White children and families. This is becoming more and more of an issue as membership within single racial, ethnic and linguistic groups is stressed in educational and political circles. Some of the issues these families face will be discussed in this chapter.

Identity

As with biracial children, the question of the interethnic child's identity comes to the fore. And, again, there are strongly held opinions that dominate the discussion. The first opinion states that, if your child has any Black heritage, he is Black (the one drop rule). Thus, if your child is Black/Hispanic, she is Black; or if she is Korean/Black, she is Black. The only exceptions to this system is for a child with enough Native American heritage to meet the blood quantum required by his nation, which differs from tribe to tribe, or if the child's phenotype (physical appearance) indicates the child can pass as non-Black.

If the child's genetic heritage does not include Black, but includes White and a parent of color, traditionally the child has been given the racial or ethnic identity of the parent of color. Therefore, if a child is Hispanic/White, she is raised as Hispanic; if Asian/ White, then he is identified as Asian. Clearly this method of identifying multiracial and multiethnic children is driven by the need to give these children a single race or ethnicity. It is also an extension of the one drop rule that historically was applied to any relationship between a White person, and a person of color (Hispanic, Native American, Asian, etc.). A biracial or biethnic child has historically always been assigned the identity of the lowest status parent. Further, it is based on a deep seated concept that the White race is somehow pure, and, therefore, cannot contain any non-White genetic heritage. It must be reiterated here that this method of categorizing mixed-race individuals is unique to the United States of America. Brazil, for example, has different labels for a range of biracial and biethnic people, depending on their racial composition.

Today many parents and professionals follow this traditional way of identifying and raising multiracial and multiethnic children. Other parents raise them according to their physical appearance. And still others raise their children as we have discussed raising biracial children - with the identity of their combined genetic, cultural and historical heritage.

Ethnic and racial pride

It is very important multiracial and multiethnic children embrace the non-White side of their heritage. A Latina/White child must feel proud about her Latina grandparents, language, history and culture. She must feel connected to her ethnic past. She may join a Mexican dance group to learn about her culture and display her pride. She may visit the country or geographic region of the origin of her Hispanic parent. And she may join the Latino student group in high school. Books, food, festivals, ceremonies, religious activities and traditions are all ways the multiracial and multiethnic child can develop pride and identity in her minority heritage.

But a multiracial and multiethnic child should not ignore, or worse yet, reject the White side of her background. Even if her parents - biological, foster, adoptive or blended - believe it is best to raise their child with the single heritage and identity of their parent of color, the child must acknowledge and embrace her White heritage. And she should never be placed is a position where one of her heritages is put down to enhance the other. Thus any activity - at school, home or in the community - that is openly anti-White or anti the child's minority heritage is very destructive to the mental health of a multiethnic child. This is also true of the multiethnic or multiracial child whose background is comprised of two or more different minority heritages.

Clearly this celebration of a child's total genetic and cultural heritage is difficult to embrace in a society that stresses group identity in a single racial or ethnic group, and often creates a sense of solidarity by stressing how different the group is from other racial and ethnic groups. For many children this need to belong to an ethnic or racial identity group is most powerful during the difficult adolescent years. There is nothing wrong with a child selecting an identity that she is comfortable with. Many single race children experiment with identities - especially in high school - jock, punk, grunge, preppie, nerd, etc. Sometimes they take these identities with them through life; often they adjust, add to them, and continue to define who they are.

What is dangerous is if a multiracial or multiethnic child totally rejects a part of her heritage and uses a hatred of part of her heritage to build up the ethnic identity she has chosen. For example, a biracial White/Latino boy who engages in hating Whites is, in fact, hating part of himself.

During middle school and high school the tremendous pressure from peers to join groups is often uncomfortable for the multiethnic and multiracial child. He is expected to reject one side of his background to fit into a singe race group; he is often accused of being too White, not Hispanic enough, disloyal or confused. At this age multiracial and multiethnic children need support from parents, teachers, school counselors and psychologists to affirm their total heritage, and not to hide or belittle part of their background.

Family support of mixed race/ethnicity children

There are three general ways families can support the healthy development of their multiethnic children. This advice applies to all multiethnic children - biological, blended, foster and adopted. These three approaches are: stress all forms of diversity; celebrate and acknowledge the child's total heritage; and never put down anyone because of their race or ethnicity.

Stress all forms of diversity. Multiracial children need to develop an appreciation for all diversity of the human condition, and the way it manifests itself - music, art, dance, language, buildings, artifacts, stories, food and traditions. They need to develop a sense that the diversity of people, their customs, and the way they view the world, is positive. They should enjoy this diversity; not learn that certain groups of people are better than others, that people must be placed into arbitrary groupings, or that all choices have a right or wrong answer.

The way to develop an appreciation of human diversity is to attend a variety of ethnic and multicultural festivals, to visit history, art and cultural museums, to have different books and magazines at home, and listen to a variety of music. Try out different foods and restaurants. Enjoy a variety of educational programs on TV. And travel! Every city has a different cultural flavor. Each city has cultural museums and landmarks. Visit Black history museums, folk art museums, Native American museums, and state and provincial parks. Visit reservations, parks, and famous landmarks. And try to visit other countries. Anything that celebrates the diversity and history of the human experience is positive. Also, accurate information about diversity is also critical. Join a folk dance group; be part of a choir; learn specific arts and crafts; join a foreign language group, and invite international students from a local college or university, or exchange program, to join in family activities. Our Christmas manger scene is made of beautiful black figurines. As I pointed out in the section about the home, our family have made a tradition of collecting - at the special times when we can afford it - items of the Black Series of Lladro porcelain figures. Other traditions we follow at Christmas include the Dutch practice of placing gifts in children's shoes, starting December 6; and trimming our tree with friends and neighbors a few days before Christmas.

When selecting a place to live, and a school for your children, make sure diversity is evident, celebrated, and viewed as a strength. But be sure that this acceptance of diversity includes multiethnic diversity, not just acceptance of single race/ethnicity.

Our children's attendance at the French school already mentioned exposed them to another language, to a variety of songs and dances, to friends from other cultures (including Africa and China), to a world view that is different from ours (including the French government's official version of European and World history), and to new customs, traditions and habits.

Celebrate and acknowledge the child's total heritage.
Through family traditions, neighborhood celebrations, customs, relatives, and stories and art work, expose your children to their total heritage. Even if you have chosen to raise your child with a singe racial identity (Black, Latino, Native American or Asian) she must be exposed to cultural activities that reflect her entire background. And she must learn to feel a pride in each strand of her heritage. Finally she must learn there is nothing unusual or wrong with a multiethnic identity.

If you have positive relationships with all your relatives, make sure your child spends time with them, and feels connected to relatives from each side of her heritage. Even if you have lost contact with one side of your child's background, do not reject that part of her, and do not bad mouth it.

As I have pointed out in other chapters, never, ever, allow your child to experience people and events that negatively portray a part of her heritage. There simply is no need to put down one group to enhance the other; multiethnic children need groups and activities that celebrate their multiethnic heritage.

Never put down relatives because of race or ethnicity.
Many families have problems with in-laws. Interracial and interethnic families are no exception. It is critical that conflicts involving relatives never revolve around the relatives' race or ethnicity. This is particularly true of families where one side of the child's heritage is not present - through divorce, separation, adoption, foster care, of because the parents were never married.

There are many single White women raising multiethnic children. Not only must these single parents make sure they don't put down the race or ethnicity of their child's father, but they must take every opportunity to expose their child to genuine, accurate examples of their father's ethnicity and culture. Maybe join a support group so your child can interact with other multiethnic and multiracial children. Interact with a variety of adults. Live in a multiethnic, integrated neighborhood and make sure your child attends an integrated child care program or school.

However, be careful not to get trapped into exposing your child to the more negative sides of her minority heritage. All cultures have negative and positive components. Carefully select interactions with your child's minority heritage that support the values and goals you have set for your unique family. If you are a middle-class family, find ways to expose your child to middle-class activities and events with a minority emphasis. Minorities, like Whites, have a diversity of professional, educational, religious and economic backgrounds. These different backgrounds provide a variability of minority values, expectations and activities. Help your child make contacts and associations with minority cultural activities that support your family's unique values.

How early childhood programs and schools can support multiethnic children

In the chapter describing how early childhood programs and schools can support biracial children and their families I discussed many ideas that also work for multiethnic children. Here are a few reminders and additional suggestions.

Teachers need to work closely with the parents of multiethnic children to determine how they support the identity of their child, how they teach their child to withstand prejudice and harassment, and how they expose him to all parts of his heritage. The teacher then needs to develop ways for the school and their classroom to support, expand and enhance these parent wishes.

Training. As I pointed out in chapter 4, any attempt by educational programs to meet the needs of multiethnic and multiracial children must start with teacher training. The training should cover two general areas: the rich and vast history of multiracial and multiethnic diversity, and how to work effectively with multiethnic and multiracial families.

There are several books that are beginning to address multiethnic history and experience: a series of books about Black-Native American history (by William Katz), two books edited by Maria P. P. Root (*The Multiracial Experience,* and *Multiracial People in America)*; Spickard's *Mixed Blood,* and several others. These should be used as a foundation for providing a historical perspective. There is also a growing number of professors teaching classes on multiracial and multiethnic issues at the university and college level. These teachers should be contacted to provide professional training. Finally there are more and more web pages that provide valuable information about the current multiracial and multiethnic movement.

Little has been written regarding supporting self-esteem and identity development in multiethnic children. However, books and article about minority identity and self-esteem can be useful, so long as the child's reference group is viewed as multiracial and multiethnic. Phinney and Rotheram's *Children's Ethnic Socialization,* is a good place to start. William Cross's work on identity development in Black children, in the same book, is also helpful. He views identity as an interaction between reference group orientation (the various groups a child identifies with) and personal identity (the way significant adults and children respond to the child).

Classic books on self-esteem (based on accomplishment, high expectations, a responsive environment, appropriate recognition, and positive interaction with peers and adults) are also helpful in developing an appropriate training for teachers. Clearly this training must also include aspects of other multicultural training -

especially those that address prejudice, harassment, equity and diversity.

Ethnic holidays. One of the difficulties of meeting the needs of multiethnic children in our classrooms is that all existing multicultural books, materials, and how-to articles only address the needs of single race students. This means that activities, ideas and approaches listed in these materials stress belonging to a single racial or ethnic group. Clearly the problem with this approach for multiethnic children is that it reinforces the societal concept that these children must select one heritage for their identity. Further, it teaches them to ignore or suppress the other parts of their heritage.

This single race approach is often used by teachers in celebrating ethnic holidays: Black History Month, Cinco de Mayo, and Chinese New Year. It is critical these holidays are celebrated in such as way that the multiethnic child doesn't feel her non-minority side must be hidden, put down, or overcome. Teachers need to talk to multiethnic families regarding how they integrate these ethnic festivals into their overall family culture. Expose children to stories about families who integrate diverse backgrounds.

Celebrating single culture celebrations does not necessarily have to be negative to the multiethnic child. But, when a biracial child is told he cannot attend Kwanza, because his mother is not Black, or when a biracial child's grandfather is ignored because he is White, then a problem does exist. Often, in recognizing the great American ballerina, Maria Tallchief, her mother is invisible, because she is White, while her father is Osage Indian. This does not help the positive self development of multiethnic children.

Use appropriate curriculum materials. The emphasis of the child care and school multicultural curriculum must be one of a world and country comprised of a variety of cultures, races, and ethnicities; and that most people throughout the world have identities comprised of several of these races and ethnicities.

As I have already discussed, books, materials, activities, field trips and classroom visitors should reinforce multiethnic and multiracial students, families and communities. Make materials if you need to. And insist that book distributors, classroom suppliers and equipment makers provide these kinds of materials.

Celebrate the school and early childhood program's diverse culture. Use the background of staff and children in your center or school to celebrate the diversity of individual heritages - language, nation of origin, ethnic, racial and tribal mixtures, and stories, legends and traditions. This can be done by students collecting oral histories, field trips, community visitors to the classroom, and parents acting as classroom resources in the center and school. The stress must be on how people integrate and combine a variety of histories and heritages to create who they are today. Look at families that combine religious, national, ethnic, racial and economic diversity to create a strong family unit. Use people who proudly talk about and celebrate the diversity of their backgrounds. Most people view their heritage as being highly diverse. And expose children to organizations in the community that celebrate various approaches to culture - such as a cultural fair, Christmas around the world, and spring and harvest festivals.

Conclusion

Children of mixed ethnic and racial backgrounds need parents who can help them explore and celebrate their total genetic and cultural heritage; and they require sensitive teachers and counselors who understand their rich background and who can support their total heritage. Supporting a child's total heritage is particularly critical during the peer-pressured middle and high school period. Programs, materials and classroom approaches need to be developed and implemented to meet these children's unique needs. Further, programs must learn to support interethnic and interracial families, while also inviting their contributions to the child care and school climate. Critical to the attempt to serve these families and their children is the way schools and early childhood programs celebrate and highlight the culture of single race students. Never must a multiethnic or multiracial child feel pressured to belittle or ignore any part of his heritage. Finally, teachers need to have specific training to prepare them to effectively work with these children and their families.

Chapter 6
Interracial and Interethnic Families: Myths and Realities

As I have discussed throughout this book, myths regarding interracial and interethnic families and their children impair our ability to raise healthy children, and to gain the support we need and deserve. Prejudice, pressure, harassment, and isolation of our families and children are all perpetuated by these myths. One of the central roles of the active interracial support groups scattered throughout this country is to explore these myths within the interracial community, and then communicate the realities of our experience to the wider population. A series of conferences, workshops, seminars and trainings have occurred throughout the country over the last 10 years to explore these issues. And publications and internet sites maintained by these support groups continue to keep important topics at the forefront of our minds. Further, interracial groups and individuals continually work with the media to present accurate information about our population. Myths must be destroyed if we are to make progress. We live in a society that has not come to terms with interracial and interethnic families, biracial and biethnic children, and multiracial people. To raise healthy biracial and biethnic children we must know and confront these myths. Further, as we concentrate on single cultural and linguistic groups when exploring inequality in this country (especially in schools), we ignore the distinct needs of children of mixed heritage.

While most of the myths and realities covered here will focus on interracial (Black/White) families, and biracial children, they apply equally to interethnic families and biethnic or multiethnic children.

Myth: Most Americans are of pure racial heritage.

A central myth about interracial families is the belief that interracial relationships are new, and therefore, questionable. Since interracial marriage is new, the myth goes, most people in this society have a single genetic and cultural heritage. Thus most Americans are of a pure racial heritage.

Reality

Interracial marriage and multiracial identity is an accepted fact in most countries of the world. Hawaii has a rich history of interracial marriage. Costa Rica and Brazil are filled with beautiful people whose physical characteristics cover a wide spectrum of facial features, skin tones, and hair textures. Brazil, Mexico and other countries have accepted interracial marriage and multiracial people for hundreds of years. This acceptance does not mean racism doesn't exist in these countries. It does. But many countries don't support the myth of racial purity.

In North American interracial marriage in colonial times was not unheard of. People of color - Native Americans, Blacks, Chinese, Filipino, Japanese and Hispanics - have a long and rich history of interracial marriage. It was common practice for Blacks during slavery to join Native American tribes for protection. Today most Native American nations require less than 100 percent Native heritage to be a member of the tribe, thus recognizing the multiracial nature of many Native Americans. Recently a series of books has been published that explore the history of Black/Native American intermarriage. And Asians in the United States of America have engaged in interracial marriage for years.

Many countries have struggled, and continue to struggle, around issues of race. For years non-Whites could not emigrate to Australia; the history of apartheid in S. Africa is well known. Japan's attitude toward people of African decent is also well documented. But the U.S. has a particular preoccupation with race. Part of this derives from our history of slavery; part because we have philosophically rejected strict class discrimination so prevalent in Europe and other countries.

As the world becomes smaller and smaller, and as barriers between nations, tribes and societies break down, intermarriage increases. There are very few local groups of people (tribes) that can claim - through social and geographic isolation- any purity of genetic heritage. The reality is that most people are multiracial or multiethnic, and intermarriage has existed since the beginning of time. The reality also is that cultural heritages have constantly been influenced by ideas and trends from other cultural groups. Culture is a dynamic exchange of ideas, languages, art, music, literature, religion and dance, habits, traditions, values and expectations.

Myth: Racial and ethnic groups are too different

A strong myth about interracial marriage is that it cannot work because people from different ethnic and racial backgrounds are just too different. The belief is that the differences between White and Black culture and the way people are raised within those cultures, will doom these marriages to failure. (This is also presumed for other ethnic groups). The assumption is based on two ideas. The first is the concept that differences between racial and ethnic groups are so great that people from one group cannot possibly understand those from another group. The current trend of insisting Black administrators run predominately Black schools, Black writers write for Black TV personalities, and Black mayors run predominantly Black cities, illustrates this concept. With the current practice of developing pride and richness in cultural groups, more emphasis is being placed on the differences between groups, rather than looking at the human experiences that transcend racial, cultural and color barriers. So today we emphasize how racial and ethnic groups differ from each other, and how people from one group cannot possibly understand the important experiences and beliefs of people from another group. "You won't understand: it's a Black thing," is an illustration of this thinking.

Secondly, there is the assumption that individuals from each group are as different from each other as one group is assumed to be collectively different from another group. For example, Blacks as a group tend to be religious, make less money than average Americans, and some live in the inner city. Whites tend to be less religious, suburban dwellers, and members - economically and politically - of the dominant group. So the myth holds that every Black is poor, lives in the inner city, is concerned about Black political issues, and goes to a fundamental church, while all his White counterparts live in the suburbs, do not go to church, and are only concerned with personal success and advancement.

Clearly, according to this myth, individuals from these two different backgrounds would find compatibility and marriage very difficult.

Finally, in this country we hold the myth that racial differences between people are greater than any other difference.

Reality: Racial groups in America are not that different

The reality is that racial groups in America are not that different from each other. They all support the basic American concepts of democracy, freedom of religion, and control of society through just laws and courts. There is a far greater difference between Blacks living in, say, Kenya, and the U.S., than between Blacks and Whites in America; or between a French man and a White, American woman; or between Black children of professional parents as opposed to children of blue collar parents. Black U.S. citizens have a diversity of historical roots. Some trace their heritage through the Caribbean; others have families whose ancestors remained in one part of the U.S.; and still others view the Trail of Tears, Asian internment camps, and herding Native Peoples into reservations as part of their heritage. For Whites, this diversity includes Ireland, Scandinavia, Russia and Italy.

This is also true of Hispanic Americans, Asian Americans, and Native Americans. The commonality between racial and ethnic groups in this country does not mean there are no differences, or that differences - especially cultural ones - are bad. Nor does it mean the search for cultural meaning and pride is bad.

What it does show is that the myth about groups being so different as to doom marriages across cultural lines is just plain wrong. Marriage between a French man and an American woman poses some cultural conflicts; Black American women who marry African men very quickly find how very different these two groups are (for example, many African men have more than one wife). Liberians who are direct descendants of American Blacks form a separate group from the native African citizens.

It is also true that a person from one cultural group does not necessarily exhibit all the characteristics of that group - especially the characteristics that we stereotypically use to set the groups apart. Not every Black person is the same; not every White person is the same; not every Hispanic is the same, and not every Native American is the same.

There is tremendous variety of people within each racial and ethnic group. People within these groups hold a variety of beliefs, enjoy a vast range of education, and have different dreams for themselves and their families. Ruth, my wife, comes from a poor, rural background. She was raised a Catholic, and has a masters degree in education. As a child she enjoyed studying English history and literature, and always dreamed of traveling to England. I grew up poor on an English farm, had a strict religious upbringing, and attended parochial schools. My college degrees are in education. We both enjoy children, travel, culture, nature, social action and interesting people. Except for our racial labels, we are highly compatible.

Despite the myth, race is not the most important (or most difficult) difference between people.

Myth: Interracial marriages fail

As a result of the myths about the incompatibility between people from different racial and ethnic backgrounds, and the belief that partners in successful marriage must have similar backgrounds, it is widely assumed interracial and interethnic marriages fail far more than marriages of people from the same racial or ethnic group. This myth is further supported by the myth that people from different racial and ethnic backgrounds marry for "unnatural reasons." For Black-White marriages these "unnatural reasons" include:

.Black men marry White women because they represent ideal female beauty. Black men have been indoctrinated into this concept of ideal female beauty by the White American media.

.Black men marry White women for status.

.Black men marry White women to get back at White society.

.White women marry Black men because they are sexually superior.

.White men marry Black women because they are exotic.

.White men marry Black women because they are good in bed.

.Whites marry Blacks because they feel guilty about White racism, and want to get back at a racist society.

.Black women marry White men to improve their economic and social standing in society.

.Black men marry White women because Black women emasculate Black men.

.Black women marry White men because Black men are sexist and chauvinist.

Clearly, as the myth goes, marriages based on these and other ulterior motives cannot succeed. And the children will suffer.

Reality: Interracial marriages are as successful and unsuccessful as other marriages

We don't have much information about the success or failure of interracial marriages. A study conducted in mid-western states showed interracial marriage to be more successful than Black-Black marriage, but less successful than White-White marriage.

Another study of interracial and inter-ethnic marriage, conducted in Hawaii, suggested interracial and interethnic marriage to be more successful than same-race marriage. This same study also found that people who married interracially were more independent than those who did not. The study indicated people willing to cross racial and ethnic barriers to marry tend to be more secure of themselves, and able to make personal choices despite societal pressure. A third series of studies suggests that, as a group, interracial partners tend to be urban, of the same religious background, and well educated.

Many contemporary interracial couples enter into a relationship fully aware that society predicts it will fail, and that their children will have problems. They know they are challenging deep seated societal taboos. These interracial couples work very hard to make sure their children have a secure home to withstand all the negative pressures of society. And many of these interracial couples are actively involved in local support groups, producing newsletters and interracial internet sites; they are also involved in impacting their children's schools and child care centers.

My wife and I have been married for over 20 years. While we have had our share of struggles, arguments and disagreements, we can honestly say none of these were based on racial differences. Most have centered around finances, jobs, raising children, parental roles and responsibilities, and differences in American and English cultural values.

Myth: Biracial children are messed up

The prevailing myth is that biracial children - in birth, foster, adoptive and blended homes - suffer greatly. The myth claims that, biologically and psychologically, mixing races produces physically and mentally weak children. A society based on single race categories and attitudes will confuse biracial children. A biracial child is torn between loyalties to each racial group. And the strong racism in this country will create tremendous psychological harm on biracial children. Finally, biracial children's unique status will produce children overly concerned with trying to fit in and trying to meet peer expectations.

The adopted biracial child, according to this myth, faces the added burden of adoption, particularly destructive if it is a transracial adoption in a White home, because his parents will not be able to protect him from the racism of the majority culture. These myths have been - and continue to be - perpetuated both in the popular media, and in much of the professional literature.

Reality: Biracial children are, as a group, as successful as other children

From a purely biological point of view, hybrids (genetic combinations of two or more distinct genetic pools of animals, birds, plants, people) are stronger than single species or single race plants or animals. They are more resistant to disease and genetic defects, and have the strengths of both genetic lines. Even pure-bred animals must have some heritage from other sources to prevent disease and problems from inbreeding. No definition of pure breeds (dogs, cattle, horses, cats) is 100%. Many purebred animals have a disproportionate amount of genetically inherited problems: Dalmatians tend to be born deaf; German Shepherds are prone to hip problems. Many new plants and animals have been deliberately produced by crossing two or more genetic families. The American Quarter Horse, the Palomino Horse, and Brangus cows are all examples.

Biracial children exhibit maximum genetic variability. This means, because they combine genes from two fairly isolated gene groups, they can show a very wide range of mental ability, along with a physical range that includes blond hair and blue and green eyes. This variability and the strengths of genetic hybrids should not be viewed as demonstrating biracial children are better than single race children; but it should be used to aggressively reject those who claim our children cannot succeed.

Clearly biracial children will show the range of problems all American children have. And - despite the sincerest of efforts by their parents and extended families - may succumb to the pressure of a racist, unresponsive society. What aggravates this problem is a lack of knowledge about the needs of interracial families and biracial children by the helping professions.

Myth: Given a choice, biracial children choose a minority identity

Because society labels biracial children with the group label of their minority parent and because society does not recognize biracial children, the assumption is that children from interracial marriages who are now adults all identify with the minority community, and view themselves as minorities. Further, it is believed all biracial children who are given a choice will choose a minority identity. This will give them a sense of group belonging, enable them to support the political struggle of minorities, and provide a reference group to help them withstand the racism of the majority culture.

Reality

While many multiracial adults do identify solely with the minority community - especially those over 30 - there is a movement in colleges around the country of multiracial students exploring their total heritage. These individuals are creating multiracial student associations, teaching classes on multiracial identity, challenging single-race university politics, and conducting research on issues surrounding biracial and biethnic identity. (Most of the studies focus on the need for biracial individuals to embrace their total identity and heritage). These college students are providing much of the dynamic leadership of the national interracial movement.

There are also older multiracial individuals, such as Ramona Douglass, president of AMEA (Association of Multi-Ethnic Americans), and Charles Bryd, of Interracial Voice, who proudly embrace their total heritage, and provide opportunities for others to explore their own identities.

What is particularly surprising about these people is that most of them were raised with the identity of only their minority parent. Further, they are exploring individual and collective multiracial issues at a time when the trend - especially in colleges and universities - is to declare loyalty, pride and political allegiance to a single minority heritage. The wish to explore their total heritage is strong enough to withstand the tremendous opposition they receive from some minority professors, student leaders, Civil Rights activists, multiculturalists, and many college newspaper writers and editors.

Myth: Only minority communities support interracial families

Shortly after the official beginning of this country interracial relationships and biracial children became very unpopular. For a variety of reasons explored elsewhere in this book, interracial families and biracial children were forced to join the minority community of their parent of color. Unless a biracial child was European-looking enough to pass as White, these individuals became part of the minority community, and saw themselves as a minority. Historically, because of racism and the one drop rule, multiracial individuals with any Black heritage have been viewed as Black, and have lived in the Black community. This is also true of multiethnic individuals.

Reality

Today there is some discussion about how well integrated these families were in their minority communities. Evidence from biracial individuals suggests sometimes these families lived on the edge of the communities. Dislike and outright hostility toward light-skinned or "yellow" children by other Blacks is well documented. At one time this dislike was based on colorism within a Black community that was jealous of people with lighter skin; later, with the rise of Black power and racial pride, preference shifted to people with more "pure" dark skin.

With the increase in integrated communities, work places and schools, and interracial marriage, many interracial families now live in integrated or White communities (especially single, female headed families). There is also an increased acceptance of interracial families by White Americans, according to several recent polls. At the same time there is an increasing opposition toward interracial families by some in minority circles. Sometimes the efforts by minorities to strengthen their own culture, history and political power, is accomplished by attacking the majority (White) culture. In my presentations about interracial marriage and biracial children I have received spotty opposition from right wing nuts, but most disagreements have come from minorities.

Myth: All cultural celebrations support and celebrate diversity

Our family recently traveled to New Mexico and visited the Pueblo Cultural Center in Albuquerque. I once lived in New Mexico, have several Pueblo Indian friends, and greatly enjoy Native culture and history. We also want our children to develop a sense of appreciation for the diverse indigenous nations in this country. Since Ruth's heritage includes Choctaw and Chickasaw, we help our children explore this part of their heritage.

The Pueblo Cultural Center is sponsored by the diverse New Mexico Native American nations, particularly the Pueblo Indians. It includes a museum, gift shop and demonstrations by Native artists and dancers. Throughout are displays of beautiful weaving, pots, art, photographs, books and religious ceremonies. Also discussions about the Native approach to the land and nature are provided and intricate models of various Indian pueblos displayed.

The museum goes out of its way to portray Spanish and Anglo influences on each tribe in a very negative light. There is even a caricature of a White tourist spending all his dollars on Indian objects (with a very negative comment written beside it). The perspective of the cultural center is one of pure race and culture. Further, it used influences from other cultures - particularly the strong Mexican and Spanish influence - in a negative way to build up the Native cultures.

There was no mention in this cultural center of the rich tradition of Native Americans and Blacks working and living together, or the positive aspects of the Spanish and Mexican influence on Southwest Indian nations. Many contemporary members of these nations have Hispanic last names; most practice Roman Catholicism- along with the Native religions of their tribe.

The museum even presented each Nation as a separate cultural and genetic entity, with no discussion of the history of intermarriage between tribes. And the museum did not help my children gain a pride in the Native American part of their heritage, or an appreciation for the art, dance and music of Native people. A child of mixed Hispanic-Native American heritage would have found a visit to this museum quite destructive. It had nothing good to say about the Hispanic culture.

Ironically, when we visit New Mexico, we also learn about and enjoy the rich Spanish American culture - going back before the colonization of the U.S. by people from Northern Europe. We love the food, and have toured the weaving villages with their unique churches along the "High Road from Taos to Santa Fe." On one such visit the old weaver proudly explained how he includes motifs in his work that were brought directly from Spain by his forefathers.

Reality. Many cultural presentations, festivals, art shows and ethnic celebrations present the view that all Americans exist within a single race and single cultural heritage

This single race or ethnicity nature of cultural festivals and exhibits poses problems for interracial families. We must expose our children to the rich diversity of cultural activities and experiences in our communities. But we cannot afford to teach our children to put down one parent's background to enhance the other parent's culture.

We must carefully select the events we take our children to, and those our schools and communities officially sponsor. One such cultural presentation is the International Folk Art Museum in Santa Fe, New Mexico. The perspective of this museum is to show that people throughout the world are joined by common human experiences and emotions. Dolls, toys, religious icons, decorative cloth and important cultural celebrations illustrate this universality. The museum also has exhibits that show how contemporary cultures are based on many different cultural influences. One exhibit shows the impact of Jewish, Christian, English, African and Arabic beliefs on Ethiopian culture (there are St. George and the Dragon motifs in their art!); another displays beautiful beadwork from

Native American Nations, Zimbabwe, Nigeria, Russia and Czechoslovakia.

A local university close to us, Denver University, annually puts on a cultural festival that presents music, dance, food, stories, songs and games from around the world. Our family loves attending this festival.

Myth: Multicultural education supports all children in our programs

There is a new wave of respect for diversity in this country. This appreciation of diversity is part of the effort to celebrate every culture and all peoples that make-up the history of this nation. It's part of the recognition that the assimilation model of America is wrong. It also encompasses a new pride and interest minorities have in their own cultural heritage. This interest in diversity is taking many different forms: in society, the media, and our schools and early childhood programs. On the surface programs and activities that celebrate a child's cultural heritage, identity and self esteem, are very welcome.

Reality: Multicultural education often does not support biracial and biethnic children

Any celebration of the diversity of people and cultures in this country should logically support interracial families and biracial children. The reality, however, is that too often they do not.

Anti-bias and multicultural education are designed to help minority students learn about their group's contribution to this country, gain pride in their heritage, and teach others about minority history, art and culture. The curriculum, books, magazine articles and teacher conferences that support multicultural education almost always take a pure race/pure culture position. That is, they teach that the minority child is the product of a unified, single minority culture (Black, Native American, Hispanic, or Asian). In fact, the language of these articles and sessions always stresses minority and disenfranchised groups, not individual members of the groups. They then teach these cultures as unique, separate entities that have no overlap with each other, or with White culture. I teach a class on diversity in the classroom for a local university. I also review books and articles on multicultural education. None of the curricular materials I use and review address the unique needs of biracial and biethnic children. None of them discuss including multiracial people in the curricular, or address the difficulty multi-racial people have experienced in the past, and biracial children experience today. A new book listing multicultural literature for children includes no books about interracial and interethnic families, or biracial and multiethnic children. Several multicultural books include activities requiring biracial children to select a minority reference group to belong to. The central problem with the traditional multicultural model is that it only looks at group belonging within traditional American racial and ethnic groups (as defined by the U.S. Census Bureau).

While this is, from an educational point of view, a neat, clean way of teaching anti-bias and multicultural education, it ignores certain realities, and views multiracial and multiethnic children as being invisible. This is the approach the Sesame Street Race Project takes in addressing diversity. When I asked the chief developer of that program why biracial children were not part of the diversity effort, I was told that it would be too difficult to include them.

Myth: The media reflects the true world of interracial families and biracial children

Unfortunately most people who are not part of an interracial family learn about us through the media. So, to them, the media represents the truth. Perception is reality.

Reality: The media perpetuate the worst myths about interracial families and biracial children

Every interracial family is aware of the media presentation of interracial issues. TV talk shows view us as freaks, newspapers continue the myth of the 'tragic mulatto' and messed-up mixed children, and magazines still debate whether interracial marriage is a good idea. Any viewing of TV talk shows quickly illustrates examples of the idea that biracial children are messed up. My family was contacted by the producer of a show on Nickelodeon. The producer interviewed each of my children for a show on biracial children, because their ages matched the demographics of the children who watch the program. However, even though the producer said my children were articulate and bright, she said she could not use them for the show, "because they had no problems."

Ruth and I have been involved in several media presentations on interracial issues - on radio, TV, and for the print media. In each case we advocated for a positive, even-handed presentation on the program. In many instances this did not occur (On one TV show the producer promised me a positive approach, then lead off the show with a member of the National Association of Black Social Workers, who strongly denounced interracial marriage).

Myth: Government policies support every form of diversity.

Since the Civil Rights legislation of the 1960s, there has been an emphasis on the rights of minorities, women and the disabled. Further, schools, colleges and businesses have strived to make sure all Americans are provided equal access to quality education and the fruits of this nation, and protected by its laws.

Reality: We use traditional U.S. racial categories to address equality

All efforts that address access and equality in this country ignore interracial families and biracial children. Cultural events, minority set asides, demographic poll collectors, minority educational conferences, newspaper articles and museum presentations, all use the single race or ethnicity approach. It's an African American art show, a Native American crafts presentation, an Irish dance festival, and a Mexican cultural celebration.

Conclusion

Interracial families must be advocates. Much of this advocacy role involves destroying myths about our population and our experiences, and challenging negative realities that affect our children. The only way to do this is to first explore these myths ourselves, and then confront them whenever we see them in friends, places of employment, our children's educational programs, the media, and society in general.

Further Reading

Here is a list of some materials about interracial and inter-ethnic families, and their children. It includes scholarly articles, children's books, and adoption materials. Books go in and out of print on a regularly basis, so I do not guarantee the availability of all the items. Some of the adoption resources are good advice for general adoption, while not necessarily supporting transracial adoption or biracial and biethnic identity development. This list is in no way inclusive; just some suggestions

For adults

Benjamin-Wardle, M. (1992). Betty Okino - a beaming biracial gymnast. *New People,* 3 (1), 8.

Benjamin-Wardle, M. (1994). Ethnic clubs exclude others. *New People,* 4 (2), 6.

Benjamin-Wardle, M. (1994). Suffer the little children. *New People,* 4 (4), 6.

Benjamin-Wardle, M. (1994). A French twist: Biracial and bilingual. *New People,* 5 (1), 6.

Bowles, D. D. (1993). Biracial Identity: Children born to African American and White couples. *Clinical Social Work Journal.* 21(4), 417-428.

Brandell, J. R. (1988). Treatment of the biracial child: Theoretical and clinical issues. *Journal of Multicultural Counseling and Development.* 16, 176-187.

Crohn, J. (1995). *Mixed Matches.* New York: Fawcett Columbine

Cross, W. (1987). A two-factor theory of Black identity formation: Implications for the study of identity development in minority children. In J. S. Phinney & M. J. Rotheram (Eds.), *Children's ethnic socialization: Pluralism and development* (pp 117-133). Newbury Park, CA: Sage.

Cruz-Janzen, M. I. (1997). *Curriculum and the self-concept of biethnic and biracial persons.* Unpublished doctoral dissertation, University of Denver, Denver, Colo.

Fish, M. J. (1995). Mixed Blood. *Psychology Today,* Nov/Dec, pp.55-80.

Forbes, J. D. (1984). Mulattoes and people of color in Anglo-North America: Implications for Black-Indian relations. *Journal of Ethnic Studies,* 12, 17-61.

Forbes, J. D. (1988). *Black Africans and Native Americans: Color, race and caste in the evolution of red-black peoples.* Oxford, UK: Basil Blackwell.

Gay, K. (1987). *The Rainbow effect: Interracial families.* New York: Franklin Watts.

Gillespie, P. and Kaeser, G. (1997). *Of many colors.* Amherst, Mass: University of Massachusetts Press.

Haislip, S. T. (1994). *The sweeter the juice: A family memoir in Black and White.* New York: Simon and Schuster.

Hall, C. C. (1980). *The ethnic identity of racially mixed people: A study of Black-Japanese.* Unpublished doctoral dissertation, University of California, Los Angeles.

Hearst, M. R. (Ed.). *Interracial identity: Celebration, conflict, or choice?* Chicago: Biracial Family Network.

Jacobs, J. H. (1977). *Black/white interracial families, marital process, and identity development in young children.* Unpublished doctoral dissertation, Wright Institute, Berkeley.

Katz, W.L. (1986). *Black Indians: A hidden heritage.* Westport, CT: Greenwood.

Kerwin, C. (1991). *Racial identity development in biracial children of Black/white racial heritage.* Doctoral dissertation, Fordham University.

Korgen, K. (1998). *From Black to biracial: Transforming racial identity among Americans.* Greenwood Publishing Group.

Ladner, J. (1984). Providing a healthy environment for interracial children. *Interracial Books for Children Bulletin,* 15(6) 13-15.

Mathabane, G. (1992). Our biracial family. *American Baby,* (July), pp.58-88.

Mathabane, M, and Mathabane, G. (1992). *Love in Black and White.* New York: Harper Collins.

Neugebauer, B. (Ed.)(1992). *Alike and different: Exploring our Humanity with young children.* (rev. ed). Washington, DC: NAEYC.

Phinney, J. (1990). Ethnic identity in adolescents and adults: Review of research. *Psychological Bulletin,* 108, 499-514.

Phinney, J. S., & Rotheram, M. J. (1987). *Children's ethnic socialization.* Newbury Park, CA: Sage.

Porterfield, E. (1978). *Black and white mixed marriage.* Chicago, Ill: Nelson-Hall

Ramirez, G., and Ramirez, J. L. (1994). *Multiethnic children's literature.* Albany, NY: Delmar.

Reddy, M. (1994) *Crossing the color line.* New Brunswick, N J: Rutgers University press.

Root, M. P. P. (Ed. 1992). *Racially mixed people in America.* Newbury Park, CA: Sage.

Root, M. P. P. (Ed. 1996). *The multiracial experience.* Newbury Park, CA: Sage.

Shackford, K. (1984). Interracial children: Growing up healthy in an unhealthy society. *Interracial Books for Children Bulletin,* 15 (6), 4-6.

Spickard, P. (1989). *Mixed blood.* Madison, WI: University of Wisconsin Press.

Sullivan, P. (1998). What are You? Multiracial families in America. *Our Children,* (February), 34-35.

Wallace, K. R. (1995). *Reflection or distortion? Student, teacher and administrator perceptions of mandatory racial and ethnic accounting.* Stanford, CA: Stanford University School of Education.

Wardle, F. (1987, Jan). Are you sensitive to interracial children's special identity needs? *Young Children*, 42(2), 53-59.

Wardle, F (1988) Who am I? Responding to the child of mixed heritage. *PTA Today*, 13 (7), 7-9

Wardle, F. (1989). Children of mixed parentage: How can professionals respond? *Children Today*, 18(4), 10-13.

Wardle, F. (1991, Winter). Raising interracial children. *Mothering*, 111-117.

Wardle, F. (1991). Interracial children and their families: How school social workers should respond. *Social Work in Education*, 13, 215-223.

Wardle, F. (1992). Supporting biracial children in the school Setting. *Education and Treatment of Children*, 15(2), 163-172

Wardle, F. (1992). Are biracial children all messed up? *New People*, 2(3), 5-15.

Wardle, F. (1994). Are biracial children successful? *Biracial Child*, 1(1) 14-17.

Wardle, F. (1996). *Multicultural education.* In: Root, M. P. P. (Ed.).*The multiracial experience.* Thousand Oaks, CA: Sage.

Wardle, F. (1996). Proposal: An Anti-Bias and Ecological Model for Multicultural Education. *Childhood Education,* 72(3), 152-156.

Wilkins-Godbee, V. (1992). First comes love, then comes marriage... *New People*, 3(2), 14.

For children

Adoff, A. (1973). *Black is brown is tan.* New York: Harper and Row.

Adoff. A. (1982). *All the colors of the race.* New York: Lothrop, Lee and Shepard.

Bonnici, P. (1985). *Amber's other grandparents.* London: The Bodley Head.

Bradman, T. (1987). *Wait and see.* New York: Oxford University Press.

Bunin, C and Bunin, S. (1976). *Is That Your Sister?* New York: Pantheon.

Davol, M. (1993). *Black, white, just right.* Morton Grove, Ill: Albert Whitman.

Fisher, I. L. (1987). *Katie Bo: An adoption story.* New York: Adama Books. (A book about a Korean adopted baby).

Harris, B. (1998). *Friendship sees no color: An award winning teen writes about growing up biracial and the interracial pen pal program he founded.* Hannacroix Creek Books, Inc.

Hoffman, M. (1987). *Nancy no size*. New York: Oxford University Press.

Jones, A. (1974). *So nothing is forever*. New York: Houghton-Mifflin.

Mandelbaum, P. (1990). *You be me, I'll be you*. Brooklyn, NY: Kate/Miller.

Marguerite, D. (1993). *Black, white, just right*. Morton Grove, Illinois: Albert Whitman.

Miller-Lachmann, L. (1992). *Our family, our friends, our world: An annotated guide to significant multicultural books for children and teenagers*. New Providence, New Jersey: R.R. Browker.

Muse, D. (1997). *The New Press Multicultural Resource Guide for Young Children*. New York: New Press.

Nash, R. (1994). *Coping as a biracial-biethnic teen*. Rosen Publishing Group.

Nye, L. (1977). *What color am I?* Abington.

Pellegrini, N (1991). *Families are different*. New York: Holiday House

Rosenberg, M. B. (1984). *Being adopted*. New York: Lothrop, Lee and Shepard.

Rosenberg, M. B. (1986). *Living in two worlds*. New York: Harper and Row.

Simon, N. (1976).*Why am I different?* Morton Grove. Ill: Albert Whitman.

Sobol, H.L. (1984). *We don't look like our mom or dad.* New York: Coward-McCann. (A photo-essay of the Levin family, which includes two Asian-American adoptees).

For adoption issues

Alstein, H., and Simon, J. R. (1991). *Intercountry adoption.* New York: Praeger

Bartholet, E. (1991). Where do Black children belong? The politics of race matching in adoption. *University of Pennsylvania Law Review,* 139,1163.

Bartholet, E. (1993). *Family bonds: Adoption and the politics of parenting.* New York: Houghton Mifflin Company.

Brodzinsky, D. M., & Schechter, D. M. (Eds.).(1990). *The psychology of adoption.* Oxford University Press: New York.

Edwards, E.E., & Radcliffe, E. (1990). *Adoption dilemma.* Communique, 7(3).

Feigelman, W., and Silverman, A.R. (1983). *Chosen children: New patterns of adoptive relationships.* New York: Praeger.

Ladner, J. (1977). *Mixed families: Adopting across racial boundaries.* Garden City, NY: Anchor Press/Doubleday.

McRoy, R. G., and Zurcher, L. (1983). *Transracial and inracial adoptees.* Springfield, IL: Charles Thomas.

Melina, L.R. (1986). *Raising adopted children.* New York: Harper and Row.

Melina, L.R. (1989). *Making sense of adoption.* New York: Harper and Row.

Player, C. (1988). Adoption: Special problems & special joys. *Growing Parent,* 16(5), 1-2

Silverman, A. R. (1993). Outcomes of transracial adoption. *The Future of Children,* 3(1) 104-118.

Simon, R. J., and Altstein, H. (1987). *Transracial adoptees and their families: A study of identity and commitment.* New York: Praeger.

Simon, R. J and Altstein, (1992). *Adoption, race, and identity.* New York: Praeger

Tieso-Battis, T.L. (1992). Surviving the triangle look. *New People,* 3(2), 9.

Tizard, B. (July, 1991). Intercountry adoption: A review of the evidence. *Journal of Child Psychology and Psychiatry and Allied Disciplines,* 32 (5), 743.

Wardle, F. (1990). Supporting the healthy development of adopted, multiracial children. *The Interracial Family Circle Newsletter,* 6(3), 11-17.

Wardle, F. (1990). Endorsing children's differences: Meeting the needs of adopted minority children. *Young Children,* 45 (5), 44-46.

Resources

Adopted Child. P.O. Box 9362. Moscow, Idaho. 83843.

Adoptive Parent Support Group. c/o AFA Inc. 3307 Highway 100, North #203, Minneapolis, MN 55422. Also materials.

Association for MultiEthnic Americans, P.O. Box 191726, San Francisco, CA 94119-1726

Anti-Defamation League. 823 U.N. Plaza, New York, NY, 10017

Brown Bear Books, P. O. Box 780-C, Englewood, NJ 07631

Claudia's Caravan, P. O. Box 1582 Alameda, CA 94501

F.A.C.E., P.O. Box 28050. Northwood Station, Baltimore, MD. 21239. (Publishes a newsletter).

Great Owl Books, 33 Watchung Plaza, Montclair, NJ 07042

Harmony Newsletter. P.O. Box 836, Effingham, IL. 62401

Interrace Magazine, and Raising Biracial Children Newsletter. P.O. Box 17479. Beverly Hills, CA. 90209

The Olive Press. 5727 Dunmore, West Bloomfield, MI 48322

Pact Press. 3450 Sacramento, Suite 239, San Francisco, CA 94118

People of Every Stripe. P.O. Box 12505, Portland, Oregon, 97212

Perspective Press. P.O. Box 90318. Indianapolis, IN. 46290

Project Race, 1425 Market Blvd., Ste 1320-E6 Roswell, GA 30076

Roots and Wings, 15 Nancy Terrace, Hackettstown, NJ 07840

Teaching Tolerance Project, Southern Poverty Law Center, 400
Washington Ave, Montgomery, AL. 36104

Internet Sites

AMEA (a national organization): www.ameasite.org/

Center for the Study of Biracial Children:
www.csbc.cncfamily.com

Interracial: www.agate.net/-wordshop/interracial.html Provides
links to interracial sites, and a list of multiracial support
groups

Interracial adoption: www.adoption.org/inter.html

The Interracial Family Circle Support Group (Wash, DC):
www.geocities.com/heartland/estates/4496

Interracial Voice: www.webcom.com/-intvoice/editor.html Links
to other sites, home pages, and multiracial news

Links to other sites: www.geocities.com/CapitolHill/Lobby5006/

Project Race: www.projectrace.mindspring.com

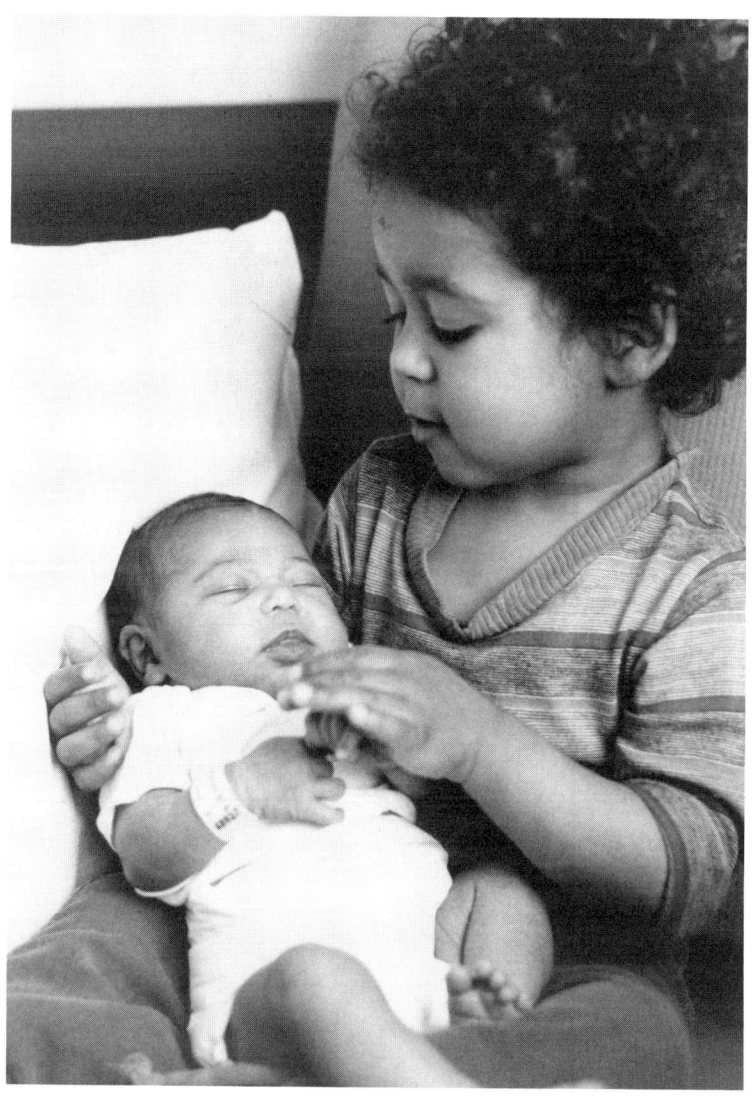